# CHIEF JOSEPH'S ALLIES

*by*
*Clifford E. Trafzer*
*Richard D. Scheuerman*

**Sierra Oaks Publishing Company**
**1992**

To Odie Faulk, with thanks

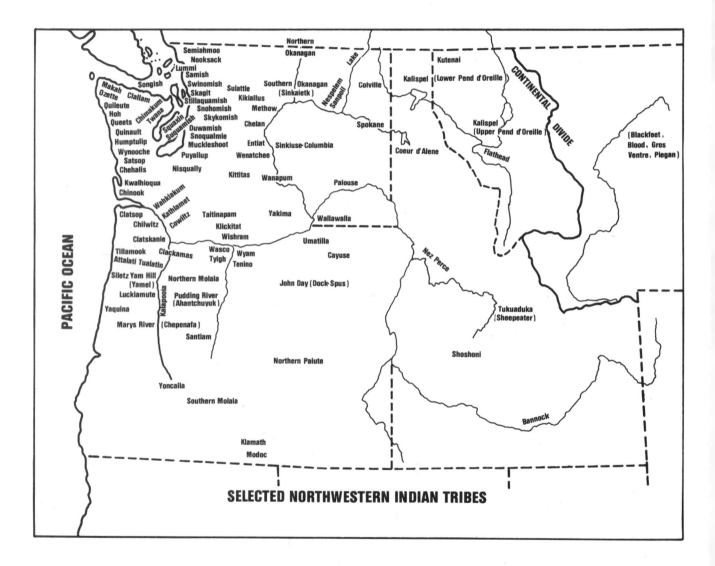

PACIFIC OCEAN

Semiahmoo
Nooksack
Lummi
Samish
Songish
Swinomish
Sulattle
Skagit
Stillaquamish
Snohomish
Skykomish
Duwamish
Snoqualmie
Muckleshoot
Puyallup
Nisqually
Kittitas

Makah
Ozette
Clallam
Quileute
Hoh
Queets
Quinault
Humptulip
Wynooche
Satsop
Chehalis

Chimakum
Twana
Squaxin
Suquamish

Northern
Okanagan

Southern Okanagan
(Sinkaietk)

Kikiallus
Methow
Chelan
Entiat
Wenatchee
Wanapum

Sinkiuse-Columbia

Yakima
Palouse

Kwalhioqua
Chinook

Wahkiakum
Kathlamet
Cowlitz

Clatsop
Chilwitz

Clatskanie

Tillamook
Attalati Tualatin

Siletz Yam Hill
(Yamel)
Luckiamute

Yaquina

Marys River

Taitinapam
Klickitat
Wishram

Wasco
Tyigh

Wyam
Tenino

Northern Molala

Pudding River
(Ahantchuyuk)

Kalapooia

(Chepenafa)

Santiam

Yoncalla

Southern Molala

Klamath
Modoc

Lake

Nespelem
Sanpoil

Colville

Spokane

Coeur d'Alene

Kutenai

Kalispel (Lower Pend d'Oreille)

Kalispel
(Upper Pend d'Oreille)

Flathead

CONTINENTAL DIVIDE

(Blackfeet,
Blood, Gros
Ventre, Piegan)

Wallawalla

Umatilla

Cayuse

John Day (Dock-Spus)

Nez Perce

Tukuaduka
(Sheepeater)

Shoshoni

Northern Paiute

Bannock

# SELECTED NORTHWESTERN INDIAN TRIBES

# Preface

Chief Joseph is considered one of the Great Indians of American history. He is best known for the Nez Perce War of 1877 and the flight of the Nez Perce to Montana. Few people are aware that a small band of Palouse Indians allied with Joseph and the various bands of non-treaty and non-reservation Nez Perce. The Palouse were led by two competent chiefs. One was *Hahtalekin* (Red Echo), a village chief with duties similar to those exerted by Chief Joseph. Second was *Husishusis Kute* (Bald Head), a holy man or *tooat* who led the Palouse in his adaptation of the old Washani religion of the Northwest Plateau.

The Palouse were drawn into the Nez Perce controversy in 1876 when General Oliver O. Howard demanded that the upper Palouse, living in villages near to the Nez Perce, move onto the Nez Perce Reservation in Idaho. The Palouse and Nez Perce met with Howard at Fort Lapwai in November of the nation's centennial year and again in May 1877. The Nez Perce and Palouse chose two religious leaders to speak for them. This was natural. Significantly, since the topic under discussion was removal from the land and since land was a subject of religious nature to Plateau Indians, it was appropriate for the Indians to select *Toohoolhoolzote* and *Husishusis Kute* to speak for them. Although Husishusis Kute never spoke, his position was well represented by Toohoolhoolzote who explained to Howard about the sacredness of the earth.

Howard disliked Toohoolhoolzote and Husishusis Kute. The "Christian General" felt that the traditional Washani religion practiced by Plateau people was savage, backward, and evil. Certainly the Washani and its religious leaders made little sense to Howard who presented his views in terms of his government's American Indian policy. Howard's order was plain and simple. He told the Palouse and Nez Perce to remove from their traditional homelands onto the Nez Perce Reservation in Idaho. Despite their objections, the Indians ultimately agreed to remove. This included those Palouse who looked to Husishusis Kute and Hahtalekin as their leaders. As a result, the upper Palouse were drawn into the web of conflict that followed the murder of whites by Indians in Idaho. When the war commenced, the upper Palouse under Husishusis Kute and Hahtalekin joined the Nez Perce. Like the Nez Perce under Joseph, White Bird, Rainbow, Looking Glass, and others, the Palouse fought and died in a gallant effort to find freedom on the Great Plains and in Canada. This is the story of the Palouse Indian involvement in the events leading to the Nez Perce War, their removal to the Indian Territory at the close of the conflict, and their ultimate return to the Northwest in that fateful year of 1885.

Several people and institutions aided us in our research. We wish to thank the librarians of the National Archives, Washington State University Library, Crosby Library, University of Washington Library, Yakima Valley Regional Library, San Diego State University Library, and the Rivera Library of the University of California, Riverside. We appreciated the help provided by John Guido, Steve Balzarini, and Joyce Justice. John Brown, Fred Bohm, and Raymond Starr read portions of the original work, offering constructive criticism and helpful advice. We sincerely appreciate the Palouse Indians who shared their oral histories with us, especially Mary Jim, Karrie

Jim, Andrew George, and Emily Peone. We thank Pamela Norman for typing the final draft of this work. Finally, we thank our parents, extended families, and children for their patience and encouragement, particularly our wives, Lee Ann and Lois.

**Clifford E. Trafzer**
**Richard D. Scheuerman**
**July, 1992**

Chief Joseph in Indian Territory.  Oklahoma Historical Society.

# THE PALOUSE WITH CHIEF JOSEPH:
## CAUSES OF THE EXILE

by Clifford E. Trafzer and Richard D. Scheurman

By the 1870s, many Indians in the trans-Mississippi West had been overrun by white miners, most of whom disregarded Indian rights. The mining frontiers in the Pacific Northwest affected native peoples as well, and the Palouse Indians had felt its impact in 1855 when Indians killed white miners in the Yakima and Palouse countries. War had resulted. The Upper Palouse and their neighbors, the Nez Perce, were not directly affected by miners until the 1860s when gold was discovered east of the Palouse Country on the Nez Perce Reservation. The gold discovery had disastrous implications for the Palouse and Nez Perce. It led to the final conquest of bands within both tribes.

As early as 1856 rumors circulated that whites had discovered gold on the South Fork of the Clearwater River in present-day Idaho. A year later a trapper named Jack Lassier reportedly found color along the banks of Orofino Creek in northern Idaho. Fear of Indian reprisals kept whites from investigating the gold rumors. However, Ellias D. Pierce was interested in the rumors. He claimed to have found gold in the Bitterroot Mountains in 1852, but he had left the region for California and British Columbia. In 1858 he returned to the Inland Northwest, ostensibly to trade with the Nez Perce. In February, 1858, Pierce and his partner, Seth Ferrell, found gold on the Clearwater River. Nez Perce Agent A.J. Cain kept the miners at bay a short time but could not hold back the gold rush.

In August, 1860, without the consent of the Nez Perce or their agent, Pierce and ten miners made a rich discovery on Canal Gulch, a tributary of the Clearwater River. News of the discovery near present-day Pierce, Idaho, soon spread among the whites.[1] The Nez Perce Treaty of 1855, signed into law in 1859, prohibited white intrusion onto the reservation without the tribe's permission. Without sufficient military support, Cain could not prevent encroachment by miners. The prospectors asserted that gold was found east of the reservation, but this was false. Cain wrote Superintendent of Indian Affairs for Oregon and Washington, Edward R. Geary, for instructions. The superintendent met with General George Wright who recommended that the Indian Bureau renegotiate the Nez Perce Treaty, permitting miners to dig for gold on the reservation.[2]

Communities of miners sprung up on the Nez Perce Reservation, including Lewiston, Elk City, and Florence. The Palouse watched a never-ending stream of merchants, miners, prostitutes, traders, gamblers, and whiskey peddlers make their way to the new El Dorado. They came in steamboats and wagons, on horseback and on foot. Whites anxiously awaited news that the government had renegotiated the Nez Perce Treaty and pressured their lawmakers to do so. On May 14, 1862, the Senate appropriated $50,000 to renegotiate a smaller reservation for the Nez Perce, and less than a year later the government created the Territory of Idaho, encompassing present-day Idaho, Montana, and most of Wyoming. Two months later, Superintendent of Indian Affairs Calvin H. Hale and two commissioners, Charles Hutchinson and S.D. Howe, traveled to Fort Lapwai to make "a new treaty, whereby the reserve was reduced . . . excluding the Wallowa, Salmon River."[3]

Some Palouse attended the Lapwai Council of 1863 to observe the proceedings. Superintendent Hale and the commissioners were wary of the Palouse, particularly after a few of them insulted the government agents. Colonel Justus Steinberger told the Palouse to leave Lapwai, but the Indians ignored the order, camping with Big Thunder, a Nez Perce chief. No doubt, the Palouse shared their ideas with the other Indians, discussed the direction of the council, and speculated about the future. On May 25, the first day of the council, Superintendent Hale bluntly informed the Indians that he wanted them to consent to a smaller reservation. Before the arrival of many Nez Perce leaders--including Joseph, White Bird, Eagle From the Light, and *Koolkool Snehee*--the Indians flatly refused to surrender their lands. Chief Lawyer, the long-time friend of the white man, reminded Hale of the Walla Walla Treaty, arguing that the Indians would not sell any lands.[4]

Superintendent Hale assured the Indians that the government wished to reduce the Nez Perce Reservation for the good of the Indians, reasoning that a smaller reservation would make it easier for the army to protect the Indians. His arguments failed to sway the Indians and the council recessed. Meanwhile, other Indians arrived who met separately with Hale, but the white commissioners fared no better with these people. Hale met individually with the Nez Perce leadership, but found Lawyer's faction of the tribe the only one willing to renegotiate the treaty.

On June 9, 1863, Lawyer and fifty-one Nez Perce men signed a treaty ceding 6,932,270 acres of land for less than eight cents an acre. None of the Palouse signed the Nez Perce Treaty of 1863. Eventually, however, the Bureau of Indian Affairs and the Army ordered them to abide by the Lapwai agreement, treating them as if they were bands of

Nez Perce.[5] Chief Lawyer and the other signers of the "Thief Treaty of 1863" sold lands that did not belong to them, but not one of the "non-treaty" chiefs, whose lands were lost, signed the document. The Palouse were totally against the treaty, and many eventually sided with Joseph, White Bird, and *Toohoolhoolzote* during the Nez Perce War of 1877.

The Palouse would have agreed with Chief Joseph's assessment that if the Indians "ever owned the land we own it still, for we never sold it."[6] The Palouse, never considered "official parties" in the treaty, were simply grouped with the non-treaty Nez Perce and considered as part of that tribe for purposes of the Thief Treaty of 1863. The Yakima Treaty of 1855 had called for removal of all Palouse Indians to the Yakima Reservation, but most refused to move onto this or any other reservation. During the three decades following the Walla Walla Council, they continued to live on their ancestral lands. The white settlement of the Palouse Country caused a schism within the Palouse communities, for a few Indians, remembering the fate of their friends and relatives who had fought Colonel George Wright, moved from the Snake and its tributaries to settle on one of the reservations east of the Cascade Mountains. They moved to the Yakima, Warm Springs, Nez Perce, and Umatilla Reservations. Others, however, remained on their lands to live as their fathers and mothers before them.[7]

Between 1863 and 1876, miners, merchants, stockmen, and farmers resettled lands that were once the sole domain of the Palouse. With the growth of the white population came demands by settlers that the non-reservation Indians be forced onto the reservations. The settlers made their demands known to legislators, military, and bureau officials. The Indians organized a loose-knit, inter-tribal confederacy based on the Washani Religion. To some degree, all of the non-treaty Indians--Palouse and Nez Perce--were influenced by the Wanapum prophet, *Smohalla*. Agents and soldiers alike worried about the "new-fangled religious delusion", labeling the religious leaders "wizards" and "magicians" who fomented trouble within the Indian communities. Among other reasons, government officials wanted to place the non-Christian Palouse and Nez Perce onto the reservation where they could be watched and Christianized.[8]

Plans to remove the non-treaties accelerated after the government decided to force Chief Joseph out of the beautiful Wallowa Valley of northeastern Oregon. Officials determined to move all of the non-treaties at the same time, and to this end, the Secretary of Interior appointed a board of commissioners to settle the Palouse and Nez Perce question. Ignoring the suggestions made by Nez Perce Agent John B. Monteith and General Oliver O. Howard, the secretary selected as commissioners David H. Jerome, A.C. Barstow, William

Stickney, Major H. Clay Wood, and General Howard. The commissioners arrived at the Nez Perce agency on November 7, 1876 with instructions to "lose no time in sending for the non-treaty Nez Perce Indians, and especially for Joseph." Six days after their arrival, they met with Chief Joseph, the great chief of the Wallowa band known to his people as *Hinmahtooyahlatkekht* (Thunder Traveling to Loftier Mountain Heights). The first Lapwai Council convened on November 13, 1876, and its outcome greatly altered the lives of the Palouse Indians.[9]

Some of the Upper Palouse attended the council where Chief Joseph was asked to give up the Wallowa Valley and move onto the Nez Perce Reservation. Joseph explained his position in terms of his religion. "The Creative Power, when he made the earth," Joseph stated, "made no marks, no lines of division or separation on it." The Indians were "of the earth", and the earth was "too sacred to be valued by or sold for silver or gold." The Indians told Howard that they would not give up their lands and would not move to the reservation. Angered by the Indian response, Howard asserted that the Indians had "denied the jurisdiction of the United States over them."[10] Joseph reflected the sentiment of all of the non-reservation Indians: "We will not sell the land. We will not give up the land. We love the land; it is our home." Upset by these words, the whites closed the council which ended unsatisfactorily for everyone.[11]

The commissioners left the council disappointed that the Indians "firmly declined" to surrender their lands.[12] Howard and the others blamed their failure on the Indian spiritual leaders or *tooats* who counseled the others not to sign treaties, surrender lands, or live on reservations--all of which the tooats considered acts against God. *Husishusis Kute* of the Palouse and Toohoolhoolzote of the Nez Perce constituted the two great holy men among these Indians. The commissioners labeled them "Dreamers," a derogatory term used in reference to all non-Christian spiritual leaders. The commissioners considered them "fanatics" who undermined the work of the government.

General Howard and Agent Monteith loathed both tooats and the traditional religious beliefs of the Indians which proved to be great obstacles to their mission. This view appeared in the annual report of the commissioner of Indian affairs. "The dreamers, among other pernicious doctrines, teach that the earth being created by God complete, should not be disturbed by man, and that any cultivation of the soil or other improvements to interfere with its natural productions, any voluntary submission to the control of the government, and improvement in the way of schools, churches, etc., are crimes from which they shrink."[13]

The commissioners' fear of the Washani leaders led them to recommend that the tooats "be required to return to the agencies . . . and in case of refusal that they be removed from further contact with the roaming Indians by immediate transportation to the Indian Territory." The commissioners further requested the military occupation of the Wallowa Valley by Howard's troops and the resettlement of the non-treaty Palouse and Nez Perce onto the reservation. The Palouse and Nez Perce were to be given "a reasonable time" to move onto the reservation, but if they refused, the commissioners wanted "sufficient force to bring them into subjection, and to place them upon the Nez Perce Reservation." As the commissioners put it: "The Indian Agent at Lapwai, Agent Monteith should be fully instructed to carry into execution these suggestions, relying at all times upon the department commander [General Howard] for aid when necessary."[14]

In January, 1877, while the Palouse wintered along the Snake River, Agent Monteith received word to move the Upper Palouse and non-reservation Nez Perce onto the reservation in "a reasonable time." Monteith asked Howard to station his soldiers in the Wallowa Valley. Monteith wanted all of the non-treaty Indians on the reservation by

April 1, an unreasonable demand due to the unpredictability of the weather and spring flooding. The agent placed a burden on the Indian leaders to convince their people that they had to move onto the reservation in order to prevent bloodshed. The Palouse leaders would have concurred with Chief Joseph's assessment of the situation. "The country they claim belonged to my father, and when he died it was given to me and my people, and I will not leave it until I am compelled to."[15]  Joseph and his brother, Ollokot, asked Monteith and Howard for another meeting. They agreed, and the second Lapwai Council commenced on May 3, 1877.[16]

Two Palouse bands attended the council, but Howard opened the meeting before they arrived. The Indians warned Perrin Whitman, the nephew of Marcus Whitman, to interpret correctly, because the council would be of importance to "coming generations, the children and children's children, both whites and Indians." Pent-up anger surfaced when one of the holy men spoke in "a cross and querulous manner," arguing that, "We want to talk a long time, many days, about the earth, about our land." Howard answered that "Mr. Monteith and I wish to hear what you have to say, whatever time it may take; but you may as well know at the outset that in any event the Indians must obey the orders of the government of the United States."[17]

During the next few days, the two major Palouse leaders, Husishusis Kute and Hahtalekin, arrived at the council. Husishusis Kute, described by General Howard as "the oily, wily, bright-eyed young chief," arrived at the Lapwai Council on May 7, "with a number of followers." Husishusis Kute led the Palouse from the village of *Wawawai* on the Snake River, fifteen miles below the town of Lewiston, Idaho. Husishusis Kute led the Palouse at Wawawai but not simply as a civil leader. The thirty-seven year old chief was also a holy man of the Washani faith who to some extent was influenced by the teachings of Smohalla.[18] According to a Nez Perce named *Peopeo Moxmox* (Yellow Bird), Husishusis Kute practiced "a religion unlike some of the others." He was one of the "new religious people" who used "a drum to beat in his worship."[19] Husishusis Kute had learned his religion first from his father, "who was an outstanding Dreamer Prophet, and spiritual man." Smohalla influenced his faith by stressing the abhorrence of reservations and control by the Bureau of Indian Affairs. Husishusis Kute "inherited both the name and mantle of his father," who had fought in the Cayuse War and had been chosen "chief of the Paloos band after the war."[20]

Husishusis Kute was not a war chief, but he had seen battle. He had been wounded by a cannon ball during Wright's Campaign of 1858. As a result of a head wound, the young warrior lost his hair, "and he told his warriors that he was going to take the name of Husishusis Kute," meaning Bald Head. Known for his sound judgement and wisdom, the Palouse selected Husishusis Kute to speak for them at the Lapwai Council.[21] The Nez Perce likely agreed to this arrangement. When Husishusis Kute arrived at Lapwai, he was disposed toward peace as was Hahtalekin (sometimes spelled *Nahtalekin)*, chief of Palus village. Known to the Palouse as *Taksoukt Ilppilp* (Red Echo), Hahtalekin was an elder, "in the buffalo-hunter class, and reckoned a brave discreet warrior."[22]

The two Palouse leaders "constituted the smallest of the 'non-treaty' groups at the Lapwai councils, where Husis-husis Kute was their spokesman." Husishusis Kute "was held in the highest esteem by all the Dreamer tribesmen" who selected him the second orator at the council after the elder Nez Perce spiritual leader, Toohoolhoolzote.[23] However, Husishusis Kute never spoke at Lapwai because of a quarrel that developed between Howard and Toohoolhoolzote. But had he spoken, Husishusis Kute would have enunciated the same doctrines as Toohoolhoolzote. Early in the council, Toohoolhoolzote crossed verbal swords with Howard, which set the hostile tone of the entire proceedings.[24]

*Ollokot* first wrangled with General Howard when he said that the Indians respected whites but they had treated him like a "dog."

He felt that "there should be one law for all."  Toohoolhoolzote, described by Howard as "broad-shouldered, deep-chested, thick-necked, five feet ten in height," reportedly "betrayed in every word a strong and settled hatred of all Caucasians." Toohoolhoolzote told Howard that he had "heard of a bargain, a trade between some of these Indians [referring to the treaty Nez Perce and the white men concerning their land; but I belong to the land out of which I came." Howard called the hold man a "cross-gained growler" who became "crosser and more impudent in his abruptness of manner." Howard explained that a "majority" of the Nez Perce had sold the original reservation and that "the non-treaty Indians being in the minority in their opposition, were bound by that agreement, and must abide by it." The non-treaty Palouse and Nez Perce disagreed, believing that no man could order them to abide by a treaty which they had not signed.[25]

In every meeting Toohoolhoolzote spoke of the "chieftainship of the earth" and explained that Indian "law" came from God which revolved around a reverence of Mother Earth. Several Indians responded angrily and defiantly to Toohoolhoolzote's word, which led Howard to intervene and cut him off.  Howard became so irritated with Toohoolhoolzote's redundant statements that he told the Nez Perce, "Twenty times over you repeat that the earth is your mother, about the chieftainship from the earth. Let us hear it no more, but come to business at once." Toohoolhoolzote announced, "You white people get together, measure the earth, and then divide it; so I want you to talk directly what you mean!"

Howard explained again that the treaty Indians had sold the land, that the law came from Washington, and that the Indians had to move onto the reservation. Toohoolhoolzote again spoke: "Part of the Indians gave up their land. I never did. The earth is part of my body, and I never gave up the earth." The general replied "that the government has set apart a reservation, and that the Indians must go upon it." Toohoolhoolzote looked fiercely at Howard and asked, "What person pretends to divide the land, and put me on it?" Howard exclaimed, "I am that man. I stand here for the President, and there is  no spirit good or bad that will hinder me. My orders are plain, and will be executed." Toohoolhoolzote wished to be left alone, warning Howard that the white men were "trifling with the law of the earth." Toohoolhoolzote concluded, announcing that, "The Indians may do what they like, but I am not going on the reservation." Howard instructed Captain David Perry to hold Toohoolhoolzote, at which point the leader responded by asking, "Do you want to scare me with reference to my body?" Perry escorted the headman to jail.[26]

The council was tense, but Howard returned and asked Husishusis Kute, Hahtalekin, Joseph, White Bird, and others if they would go "peaceably on the reservation, " or if they wanted him "to put them there by force?" None of the Palouse or Nez Perce, except Toohoolhoolzote, favored war which the Indians felt would result in disaster. One by one, the leaders consented to move to the Nez Perce Reservation, including Husishusis Kute and Hahtalekin. Chief Joseph assessed their situation saying: "We were like deer. They were like grizzly bears."[27]

The Palouse and Nez Perce agreed to move, and to this end Husishusis Kute, Hahtalekin, and the Nez Perce chiefs toured the Nez Perce Reservation, selecting lands onto which they would move. Howard wrote that "Hush-hush-cute will go to the land along the Clearwater, just above the agency."[28] For religious reasons, some of the non-treaty Nez Perce wanted to be located next to Husishusis Kute where "nobody will interfere with our worship."[29] Chief Hahtalekin chose lands nearby the other Palouse. Howard told the Palouse to relocate on the Clearwater within thirty-five days, an unreasonably short time for the Palouse leaders to convince their people to move, gather their belongings, round up their herds, and move to Lapwai. Howard and Monteith feared that Husishusis Kute would use his position as a tooat to rally the Indians and incite violence.[30]

Howard told the Palouse that if they "let the time run over one day, the soldiers will be there to drive you on the reservation, and all your cattle and horses outside of the reservation at that time will fall into the hands of the white men."[31]  This added insult to injury, but neither the Palouse nor the Nez Perce could stand against the United States Army.  At the end of the meeting on May 14, Howard handed each Indian leader a "protection paper," assuring them safe passage from their homelands to the reservation.  When Howard handed the protection paper to Husishusis Kute, the Palouse refused it "with a curt explanation."  He told Howard, "I do not want it! I might get it dirty!"  Husishusis Kute made this remark because "the proud Paloos Chieftain" was "incensed at the penury of the time limit for their removal."[32]

Howard and Monteith considered Husishusis Kute's remarks an insult.  The remark so offended Howard that he withdrew the paper, explaining later that Husishusis Kute "was the only Indian who, at this time, betrayed any symptoms of treachery.  His protection papers were withheld on account of it, and given to the agent to be presented to him when the agent should be satisfied of his good intentions."  Husishusis Kute upstaged the general, and the other non-treaty Indians laughed at his remark.[33]

Husishusis Kute and Hahtahlekin returned to the Snake River to tell their people of the Lapwai Council and the decisions made there, news which made their "hearts sink to the ground."[34] Because of the nature of Palouse society, each family and band decided for themselves whether they would move onto the reservation or remain in their homeland. In order to avoid bloodshed, Hahtahlekin chose to move onto the reservation. Some Palouse went to other reservations to live with relatives, while others defied the government altogether. A few Palouse prepared to move onto the Nez Perce Reservation immediately, joining a large gathering of non-treaty Nez Perce on the Camas Prairie. In west central Idaho, the Indians met to gather roots, race horses, and visit friends and relatives.[35] While most of the upper Palouse prepared to move onto the banks of the Clearwater River, Howard convened a meeting with some of the Lower Palouse living on the Snake River between Palus and Quosispah, located at the junction of the Snake and Columbia rivers.

Among the Lower Palouse, *Thomash* commanded great respect as a Washani holy man. He lived at the village of *Sumuyah* (near Fishhook Bend on the Snake River) with fifty followers, including his brothers and relatives of *Tilcoax,* the famed Palouse war chief. In May, 1877, Howard summoned Thomash to a meeting. The Lower Palouse chief did not trust white men, and since his youth, he had boasted that because of his *somesh* (spirit power), no shackles or jails could hold him and no bullet could penetrate his body. In 1856 the Palouse headman had been captured by volunteer troops under Colonel Thomas Cornelius, and as a young man, Thomash had learned the ways of the whites.[36]

Howard convened a council among the Lower Palouse, Cayuse, Walla Walla, and others. After some consideration, Thomas attended the council and joined Young Chief of the Cayuse, *Homily* of the Walla Wallas, and Smohalla of the Wanapums. Over three hundred Indians "freshly bedecked with paint and feathers" met Howard near the crumbling walls of old Fort Walla Walla. Howard characterized Thomash as "a refractory chief" whose people "wanted peace, but they desired much more to roam at large whenever and wherever they pleased." The general believed that before the Lower Palouse moved to any reservation, they would observe the Upper Palouse and Nez Perce situation, knowing that "should they alone [the Lower Palouse] precipitate war . . . they would soon be annihilated."

During the council, Howard and Umatilla Agent W.A. Connoyer explained the benefits of reservation life. The Indians convinced Howard and Connoyer that most of the Indians, except for the Palouse, had come to the council "with apparent good feelings." Howard reported that Thomash "was wild and fierce to the last," and he later recalled that Thomash "wanted to know why I had been sending troops to Wallowa, and denounced the action and wishes of the United States government in unmeasured terms." The chief and his people stormed out of the parley, returned up the Snake River "making better time than the steamboat."[37]

Andrew Pambrun served as Howard's interpreter, and when Thomash spoke out and bolted the council, Pambrun offered to "tame him a little" by incarcerating the boastful leader. Given the volatile situation, Howard refused and instead convened another meeting at Fort Simcoe on June 8. This council was attended by "all the Indians far and near, north of the Columbia River." Thomash, Moses, Smohalla, and the Yakima, *Calwash*, attended the council. After formal introductions, Howard delivered a brief address striking at the heart of the issue: "The government requires that you shall all come on this [the Yakima] or some other of its reservations."

Howard announced that "the commander of the military forces will enforce this requirement." On Monday, June 10, Moses and Smohalla agreed to move to a reservation. Finally, Thomash, "a spare, tall man afflicted with a nervous trembling," arose to say that he would "go to the Umatilla reservation by the first of September." When the chiefs agreed to relocate to a reservation, Howard left the council for Fort Lapwai to supervise the Nez Perce relocation. He arrived at the post as a messenger entered the garrison with news of great importance.[38]

While Thomash met Howard, a few Upper Palouse and several Nez Perce gathered at Tolo Lake, located six miles east of Grangeville, Idaho.  The purple flowers of the camas covered the prairie like the nap of a carpet, and the people dug spring roots to dry before moving onto the reservation.  While the men and women prepared to move, several young people fretted over their own fate and that of future generations.  Depressed over the situation, some people drank to excess.  One young man, *Wahlitis,* joined in a horse parade and afterwards rode carelessly about camp, permitting his horse to trample roots that had been laid out to dry.  A man and a woman who had gathered the roots rushed out, scolding Wahlitis and telling him that if he thought himself a great warrior, then he should avenge his father's death.  The previous year, Larry Ott had murdered Eagle Robe.  Angered by the rebuke, the young man accepted the challenge, deciding to kill his father's murderer.

Wahlitis, *Wetyetmas* (Swan Necklace), and *Sarpsis Llppilp* (Red Moccasin Tops) raided white settlements along the Salmon River, killing three white men and wounding another.  The young men did not find Ott, but they tasted revenge.  Word of their deeds quickly spread among the whites and Indians, and the next day other Indians joined Wahlitis. Small forces swept down on the Salmon River settlements again, triggering a tragic conflict known as the Nez Perce War. Young Palouse probably did not join the original war parties, but the actions of these groups influenced the course of Palouse history.[39] The raids caused great anxiety in the white and Indian communities. Nez Perce leaders moved the people off the Camas Prairie into White Bird Canyon, while Husishusis Kute elicited support among the interior Indians on behalf of the non-treaty Indians.

At the outbreak of the Nez Perce War, several bands of Palouse camped with hundreds of other Indians on a camas meadow near the Coeur d'Alene Mission. The Coeur d'Alenes had no agent, and many Indians rendezvoused to dig roots, race horses, and discuss recent events. The Catholic missionaries and Christian Indians living near the mission were "much bothered" by the "unruly" Indians of the Washani faith. The Jesuits labeled these Indians, "pagan dreamers" and they feared that these unwanted elements would cause violence. For this reason, *Seltice*--a Christian and Coeur d'Alene leader-- prohibited all of the Indians from drinking or gambling. The prohibition upset many Indians, but they reached a compromise after three Spokane Chiefs suggested that all who did not wish to abide by the restrictions should move west to Elposen, located nine miles off the reservation near present-day Tekoa, Washington.[40]

News of the Salmon River raids reached some Palouse as they resettled at *Elposen*. Many Palouse were sympathetic to the Nez Perce cause, and some advocated active support of their neighbors. Seltice stood firmly against joining, saying that the Coeur d'Alenes "were friends of the whites, and we will have nothing to do with the murderers." Some of the younger men among the Palouse bands rode off to engage white settlers in the Palouse Country, but the warriors found most of the cabins empty. When whites learned of the Salmon River raids, they sought refuge in the small frontier towns.

Farmers east of Colfax, Washington, heard about the raids when a rider from Lewiston, Idaho, rode into a camp meeting on Saturday, June 16, near present-day Elberton. The assembly was "thrown into a fervor by the news that the Indians were assuming hostile positions in the district east of us toward Lewiston." The messenger reported that one family near Lapwai had just been massacred and that "others had been murdered without mercy." Cooler heads prevailed, and the attending preacher offered prayers of comfort to the assembled families. Although this initial report "did not have much effect" on the congregation, they dismissed to their homes with anxious feelings.[41]

Unsubstantiated rumors about hostile Indians floated about like ominous storm clouds. From Lewiston, Idaho, to Dayton, Washington, white settlers sounded the alarm that the interior Indians had launched a general uprising. A Lewiston newspaper reported that the Nez Perce and Upper Palouse were to be joined by "several hundred fighting men from the different bands who have hitherto been considered friendly."[42] The citizens of Colfax received word that "400 Indians, more or less, traveling in a body had killed 80 persons on the Clearwater, and were coming toward Colfax, sweeping all before them."[43] White settlers rushed to the nearest town, as rumors circulated and "terror ruled supreme."

Volunteer troops organized and towns readied for full-scale attacks. Women and children were sequestered in schoolhouses, mercantile stores, and saloons, preparing for a siege. Men gathered their weapons and took positions to protect their friends and families. Men dug fire pits and made preliminary plans. Sixty wagons of panic-stricken people fled their farms and stock to seek refuge in a Colfax schoolhouse. Citizen Frank Bowman, Carl Floyd, and George Sutherland acted as guards on the south side of Colfax, but neither these guards nor those on the north end of town saw any Palouse. However, one sentry fired a round at a phantom Indian. The white settlers feared all of the Indians of the region, believing that Joseph had sent runners to the "Pallouse, Spokane, Columbia River and Umatilla Tribes." Some believed that all of the interior Indians would soon join the Nez Perce and Upper Palouse "and that they would capture the whole country."[44]

News of the war spread like a dreadful grassfire, and whites everywhere huddled together for protection. At Palouse City the citizens cut 480 wagonloads of pine and fir poles, using them to build a sturdy stockade around the Ragsdale Store. The blockhouse measured 125 feet in circumference and housed 200 people. The women and children took up residence on the second floor of the store, while the men camped in tents outside the store but inside the walls of their fort. Local residents organized a volunteer company under the banner of the "Palouse Rangers," and they elected Captain J.M. Greenstreet their commander.

At the same time that the citizens of Colfax and Palouse City prepared for an Indian attack, the residents of Pine Creek, Farmington, Leichville, Spangle, and Four Mile Creek (near Moscow, Idaho) made similar fortifications and formed local militias. Whites living in the present-day Orecho District along the Snake River reportedly learned from local Palouse Indians of potential danger. Many whites had gathered at *Penawawa*, Washington (a former Palouse village), to ship their bales of wool on a steamboat of the Oregon Steam Navigation Company, and while they waited for the boat, they constructed a fort out of the wool bales, complete with gun portals and corner standouts. The herders remained there a few weeks, but the impending attack never materialized.[45]

Every community in the Palouse Country received conflicting reports and exaggerated rumors of hostile Indians. David Bowman and James Tipton of Colfax scouted the Washington and Idaho border, returning to Colfax to report "that the Indians [Palouse and Nez Perce] had not crossed the Clearwater but were going toward the mountains." Another scouting party led by James Perkins returned to Colfax with similar news about the hostile Palouse and Nez Perce.

While the citizens breathed a sigh of relief after learning that the hostiles had headed east over the Bitterroot Mountains, they worried over a report from Bowman and Tipton that "the Coeur d'Alenes were going to break out the next day, kill all the people at Mr. Howard's stockade [located on the Idaho border], and send a detachment to Colfax to massacre all the people there."

The whites feared this rumor since Bowman and Tipton had received the intelligence from an Indian who had recently been at the Coeur d'Alene Mission. Settlers at Pine Creek had heard similar reports from James D. Gralen and Melville Choate who had visited the mission and found the Indians "in a high state of excitement." They learned no other substantive information and returned to Pine Creek.

On their journey across the Palouse Hills, they saw two Indians armed with rifles, but the Indians simply rode off.[46]

Father Joseph Cataldo of the Coeur d'Alene Mission worried that peaceful Palouse, Spokane, and Coeur d'Alene would be drawn into a needless and bloody conflict. For this reason, he penned a letter to the *Lewiston Teller* informing whites that "the Indians are all quiet up on the Hangman Creek, although a good many of the Nez Perce and Palouse are there." The same day, the *Walla Walla Union* reported five hundred Indians on Hangman Creek but that there were "no hostilities there yet." After conferring with the Indians in the northern Palouse Country, Cataldo became concerned, because the Indians there feared a possible attack by white settlers. Native Americans had good reason for concern, since the whites had mobilized their forces in reaction to "the harrowing, horrible details of the result of trusting the honor of the Indians." According to the editor of the *Walla Walla Union*, "No live Indian can be trusted", since "ninety-nine hundreths of the people of this country" favored extermination of all Indians. Before another war broke out, Cataldo sought to quiet the dangerous direction of events on the Plateau.[47]

The Jesuit told Bowman and Tipton of his concerns after they arrived at the mission on another scout of the region. The citizens of Colfax, Bowman and Tipton told Cataldo, remained in near hysteria, fearing attacks from the Palouse, Nez Perce, Coeur d'Alenes, and others. Cataldo introduced Bowman and Tipton to Chief Seltice and two Palouse chiefs, *Ususpa Euin* and *John Fla.* Ususpa Euin, a Palouse headman from the village of *Almota* on the Snake River, and John Fla, a leader from the Snake River, explained their peaceful dispositions. Both men wished to return to the Snake, but both feared being attacked by the white settlers. Ususpa Euin, an imposing figure six feet tall with heavy brows and long black hair, told Bowman and Tipton that the Palouse had "come up here to run horse races and our women are out digging camas. By and by they will all come in and we will go home. We don't want war for many reasons and you don't want any war." The Palouse headman assured the two white men that his Palouse band wanted "to live together [with white people] and be friends."[48]

Following a brief speech by Fla, Chief Seltice spoke, asking "why the white people had all gone to Colfax and were building big houses." It appeared to the Coeur d'Alene that whites wanted war. When Bowman and Tipton assured the chiefs that the whites did not want war, the Indians asked them to tell the settlers to return to their homes. At the urging of Father Cataldo, the chiefs dictated letters, sending them to the towns explaining that their bands wanted peace. Ususpa Euin wrote that his Palouse had no intention of giving "trouble to any white." He prophetically stated that "If Joseph and his friends make war against the whites, that war will finish them." Fla confirmed that his "heart is always good, and the whites have nothing to fear from me, or my people." The letters helped quiet the region. Bowman and Tipton returned to Colfax where the local newspaper reported that the "Indian scare" had actually turned out to be "the grand Palouse humbug."[49]

Nevertheless, trouble stirred among the Coeur d'Alene and Palouse. Agents of Husishusis Kute had moved among the Indians, attempting to rally support for the war. Some Palouse still wished to return to their homes on the Snake, while others thought it wiser to move north to the Spokane country. To reassure the whites that the Palouse and Coeur d'Alene wanted no trouble, Seltice wrote General Howard informing him that "the Palouse Indians were quiet here amongst us digging camash as of old; now a report came of late, telling to run away from amongst us, because the soldiers would come and drive all Catholic Indians away." Seltice said that while he put no faith in these rumors, his friend, "Chief Ususkein wanted to move off" as did the Nez Perce chief, Three Feathers. The priest blamed these stories on a campaign designed by Husishusis Kute, to "turn the good feelings of our Catholic Indians" against the whites and join the warring factions.

Husishusis Kute had tried to unite the non-committed Indians of the region. He believed that some Palouse had been enticed by the" American religion," and he sought their return to the traditional way of the Washani. Father Joset reported that some Palouse, "*Skwelkeel* or his brother," had visited the Indian camps near the mission carrying Husishusis Kute's message.[50]

Unlike some of the Palouse and Nez Perce leaders, Husishusis Kute viewed the outbreak of hostilities as a pretext to unify the tribes in a crusade against all whites and their religion. His efforts failed to enlist the kind of response for which they had hoped. The Palouse bands under Ususpa Euin and Fla either returned to their river homes or fled to the Spokane Country where another group of Palouse under Chief *So-ie* camped far from harm's way. Emissaries from the disparate bands prompted the influential Spokane chief, *Sgalgalt*, to write General Howard, reassuring him that the Spokane would not join the fighting. He assured Howard that the Spokane and Palouse would not loot the deserted homes of surrounding settlers who fled to Spokane Falls or the nearest frontier town.[51]

In mid-June, 1877, Chief Thomash of the Lower Palouse arrived in Waitsburg, Washington, with five Palouse from their Snake River home of *Sumuya*. General Howard had feared that Thomash might be drawn into war if the Nez Perce took the initiative, but the headman opposed the war. Dozens of curious whites watched as the six Palouse rode into the town and listened as Thomash assured everyone that "all the Indians with the exception of a portion of the Nez Perce tribe, are peaceable disposed, and anxious to maintain friendly relations with the whites." Smohalla remained equally cordial, but many Indians remained "alarmed for fear the whites could turn against them." A local correspondent for the *Walla Walla Union* urged everyone to "act sensible and prudent, and deal justly with the Indians."[52]

With Husishusis Kute's envoys spurned by the leaders of virtually all the interior tribes, some hostiles developed a more direct method to embroil the tribes in the crisis. By June 22, individuals and families who had gathered in the Pine Creek area during the "Indian scare" returned to their homes. One of the settlers, John Ritchie, rode horseback to his cabin near *Elposen* on Hangman Creek. The day after returning, two warriors--Palouse or Nez Perce--rode into the Elposen Indian camp announcing that they had killed two whites. According to their version, they had been accosted by whites and had defended themselves in a gunfight. Fathers Cataldo and Joset identified the young Indians as sons of a respected Palouse Indian named *Etelschen* whose people belonged to a "small band of Indians on the Snake River." After creating a sensation at Elposen, the two brothers rode southeast about ten miles to the camp of Coeur d'Alene Chief *Konmoss* where their father had camped.[53]

Upon hearing the report, both Chief Konmoss and Etelschen condemned the act, informing the priests that the Indians did not want a repeat of the tragic events that followed the killing of two miners near Colfax nearly two decades earlier. On the evening of June 23, Chief Konmoss dictated a letter to Father Joseph Giorda, informing the white settlers that "two Indians from between Palouse and Nez Perces River came to his camp telling that they have attacked and shot at two white men." The Jesuit believed that one of the whites had been killed.

The Indian leaders realized that the killing might trigger a war, and Father Giorda reasoned that such an act in Coeur d'Alene territory would constitute what "in Indian policy would be an act of hostility on their part against the whites; had the Coeur d'Alenes looked upon it indifferently it would have been taken as a sign that they were at heart with the rebels."[54] Moreover, the deed would give credence to articles circulating in the Walla Walla newspapers "that the Coeur d'Alene Indians had joined Joseph's band of outlaws, that they numbered several hundred warriors; and that they were marching down from Hangman's Creek, killing and destroying as they came."[55]

Chief Seltice confiscated the horse brought in by the two young Palouse, returning it to the whites with a letter stating that it had been taken by "an Indian of the Snake River; and that the owner was robbed and killed; the thief says he murdered the white man."[56] The news created a sensation among the farmers at Pine Creek, where whites recognized Ritchie's horse. Two white men and an Indian rode to Ritchie's place and found that the settler had been struck in the forehead with an axe and shot in the breast with "the ball ranging downward." It appeared as though Ritchie had been murdered, and news of this finding had an immediate impact in both the white and Indian communities. The whites scrambled back to their sanctuaries and the Indians followed suit. As for the Palouse, they feared both the whites and the Coeur d'Alene. Most Palouse moved north to the Spokane Country in order to avoid danger.[57]

Once again whites living in the Palouse Country feared all Indians, believing that hostiles had camped "a short distance from us" and had "taken up arms and have murdered Men, Women and Children in cold blood." The whites wanted retribution for the Ritchie killing, stating that "in the present condition of the Public Mind many Innocent persons may suffer and much property may be destroyed."[58] Although outraged by the killing, the whites did not attack any of the Indian camps, and a calm slowly settled across the Palouse Country.

Some Palouse who had fled northward professed their friendship with the whites, while others proved hostile. Some of the younger men, swayed by the arguments presented by the messengers of Husishusis Kute, joined the Palouse who had moved off the Snake River and onto the Clearwater. Husishusis Kute had favored hostilities with the whites since the early stages of the Nez Perce War, but no evidence exists suggesting that Hahtalekin wanted war. Indeed, after the raids on the Salmon River, Hahtalekin returned to the Snake River and later moved his people onto the reservation. Yet, Hahtahlekin soon joined forces with the hostiles in response to an unprovoked attack on Looking Glass' village.[59]

When news of the Salmon River raids reached the Nez Perce camp on the Camas Prairie, the Indians feared that war would result. Anticipating the movement of troops against them, Joseph and Ollicot directed their people to join ther other hostile Nez Perce and move into White Bird Canyon. Full scale war commenced on June 17, 1877, when troops under Captain David Perry engaged the Indians in the Battle of White Bird Canyon. The army suffered heavy losses and were driven from the field. Shortly afterward, General Howard assumed field command, and the war commenced in e arnest. While the Nez Perce engaged the soldiers north of Salmon River, some Palouse and Nez Perce sought refuge from war on the Clearwater River. Nez Perce conducted nearly all of the early fighting, although some Palouse fought with Joseph's band. One such Palouse, *Kosooyeen* (Going Alone), "was reputed by his compatriots a brave warrior and adroit scout." A favorite among the Indians, Kosooyeen belonged to Hahtalekin's band. He fought with the Nez Perce along the Salmon River and had spied on the soldiers for Chief Joseph.[60] According to Yellow Wolf, a Nez Perce warrior and nephew of Joseph, Hahtalekin "did not want war." But the Palouse chief joined the war after Captain Stephen G. Whipple attacked the camp of Looking Glass. Some Palouse, likely including Hahtahlekin, were related to the Looking Glass family. When word reached Hahtahlekin that his friends and relatives had been attacked, his band joined the conflict.[61]

Most Palouse warriors joined forces with the Nez Perce in mid-July, 1877, when the various Indian bands met on Weippe Prairie. The chiefs held council to determine what course of action to take. Looking Glass, Hahtahlekin, Five Crows, Rainbow, Toohoolhoolzote, and Five Wounds favored crossing the Bitterroot Mountains and living with the Crows in Montana. Reluctant to leave the Wallowa for Montana, Joseph and Ollicot decided to do so after learning that most chiefs favored the move. Looking Glass, the strongest advocate of the move to the Crow Country led the Indians. Hahtalekin and Husishusis Kute deferred to Looking Glass, believing as many did, that aside from

Toohoolhoolzote and White Bird--the older statesmen of the non-treaty Nez Perce--Looking Glass had the greatest war experience. Looking Glass led the Indians from Idaho to Montana across the Lolo Pass, believing that once they left Idaho, they would no longer be harassed by soldiers.[62] The Palouse and Nez Perce encountered little trouble from the soldiers, traveling across the Bitterroot Mountains before turning south through the Bitterroot Valley. They continued to the basin of the Big Hole River where they fished, hunted, and cut lodge poles at this sacred site. Tired from their arduous journey, the Indians rested for the first time in many weeks, dancing and singing in celebration of their escape.[63]

Some Indians objected to remaining at the Big Hole, particularly after *Wootolen,* a man of "strong powers", dreamed that soldiers were near. Some Indians wanted to backtrack through the Bitterroot Valley, but Looking Glass spoke against the plan. Angry at the lack of support for the scouting party, Five Wounds remarked pointedly: "All right, Looking Glass. You are one of the Chiefs! I have no wife, no children to be placed fronting the danger that I feel coming to us. Whatever the gains, whatever the loss, it is yours."[64] On August 9, 1877, the dream of Wootolen came true, when soldiers under Colonel John Gibbon, commander of the Montana District, attacked the Indians at the Big Hole. Gibbon surprised the Indians, and his soldiers crawled close to the Indian camp in the pre-dawn hours of that summer morning.[65] As Hahtalekin rode out to check the horse herd, he was gunned down. The soldiers fired several shots into the Indian camp, before the soldiers charged the encampment. Chief Hahtalekin sounded a warning, as the women and children rushed out of their tipis in the face of "fierce fighting."[66] As Wounded Head put it: "Hand to hand, club to club. All mixed up, warriors and soldiers fought. It was a bloody battle." Bullets showered down on the Indians like hail, and gunfire ripped "the tepee walls, pattering like raindrops."[67]

In the heat of the Battle of the Big Hole, several warriors fell, including Palouse. Chief Hahtalekin died during the fighting as did his son, *Pahka Pahtahank* (Five Fogs). According to Yellow Wolf, Pahka Pahtahank fought alone on the banks of the Big Hole River wearing a white King George blanket. "Aged about thirty snows, he was of an old-time mind. He did not understand the gun. He was good with the bow, but had only a hunting bow." Yellow Wolf thought to himself: "If he [Pahka Pahtahank] had good rifle, he could bring death to the soldiers."[68] The young Palouse warrior died protecting the camp, and Yellow Wolf recorded the event: "He was just in front of his own tepee. Soldiers were this side, not far from him. He stood there shooting arrows at the enemies." The soldiers fired repeatedly at the Palouse warrior who dodged the bullets by stepping "about a little," but all the time continuing to fire arrows at the soldiers. "Three times those soldiers fired and missed him. The fourth found him."[69]

Twenty minutes after the battle commenced, Gibbon took the Indian camp. The Nez Perce and Palouse had been cut to pieces, but White Bird and Looking Glass rallied the warriors and counter-attacked, showering the soldiers with bullets and driving them from camp. The Indians captured a mountain howitzer and a mule loaded with two thousand rounds of Springfield rifle ammunition. Men and women alike fought and kept the soldiers at bay until the others escaped the Big Hole during the night of August 10. Approximately fifty-four women and children died in the battle, while thirty-three men perished. Joseph and Ollicot lost their wives during the fight, and several noted warriors died, including Hahtalekin, Pahka Pahtahank, Rainbow, Wahlitis, and Sarpsis Llppilp. Looking Glass survived, but much of his power dissolved after the Big Hole disaster. Lean Elk emerged as the major chief, and he and others led the people on a trying journey through western Montana, eastern Idaho, and the Yellowstone National Park of northwestern Wyoming.

In their escape to the open plains of central Montana, the Indians skirmished with Howard's troops at Camas Meadows and eluded the command of Colonel Samuel D. Sturgis, assigned to surprise the Indians along the Clark Fork River. Under orders from

Howard, Colonel Sturgis engaged the warriors at Canyon Creek, but the Indians escaped. Looking Glass had bragged of his friendship with the Crow, claiming that they would aid the people, but when the chief visited the Crow, they gave him an insulting rebuff. The summer before the Crow had scouted for Colonel George Armstrong Custer, and they wanted nothing to do with the Nez Perce War. When the Palouse and Nez Perce headmen learned that the Crow would not help them, the leaders decided to escape to Canada. Some of the people hoped that Sitting Bull would provide support, but their hopes ended when the exiled Sioux never arrived.[70]

Following the Battle of Canyon Creek, Sturgis sent a rider to Tongue River Cantonment with a message from Howard to Colonel Nelson A. Miles, asking the colonel to cut off the Indians from the east. Miles longed for such an opportunity, and he moved quickly to act on Howard's request. With a combined force of approximately four hundred men, including thirty Sioux and Cheyenne warriors, Miles crossed the Missouri River, racing northward toward the Canadian border to intercept the fleeing Indians. Of this the Palouse and Nez Perce knew nothing, believing that the only soldiers following them were those under General Howard.

With the army far behind, Looking Glass rode about the tired and wounded Indians urging them to slow down. The Grand Mother

Country--Canada--was not far off, he argued. The Indians had ample time to escape. After leaving the Missouri River, the Indians camped early each day to rest. On the afternoon of September 29 the Indians camped in the valley of a small tributary of Milk River called Snake Creek. The creek lay between the Bear Paw and the Little Rocky Mountains--approximately forty miles from the Canadian border--forty-eight hours from freedom. There they rested for two nights while the soldiers under Miles closed in on the unsuspecting Palouse and Nez Perce.[71]

In a cold rain and a pea soup fog, Sioux and Cheyenne scouts found the Palouse-Nez Perce camp. Shortly afterwards, Miles charged and a bloody battle ensued. The soldiers and warriors fought at close quarters, and some of the women and children fought with digging sticks and butcher knives. Miles lost many men and officers because of the deadly marksmanship of the hostile warriors. For this reason the colonel laid siege to the Indian position with Hotchkiss and Napoleon guns. Some of the Indians, including Yellow Wolf, White Bird, and the twelve-year old daughter of Chief Joseph, left the battlefield for Canada. Most of the Indians took cover from the gunfire and miserable weather which brought five inches of snow and cold winds. On October 1, Miles raised a white flag in his camp and called out to Joseph requesting a parley. The Indians met in council to discuss a cease-fire, but missing from the gathering was Ollicot, Toohoolhoolzote, and Lean Elk, all of whom had been killed during the first day of fighting. Looking Glass and White Bird feared that if the Indians surrendered, Howard would hang them, just as Colonel George Wright had done in 1858. Tom Hills, a Nez Perce interpreter, visited Miles and received an assurance that Joseph would not be harmed. As a result, Joseph met Miles halfway between the two camps.[72]

Joseph and Miles talked of surrender, and Miles demanded that the Indians lay down their arms. Joseph suggested that half of the firearms would be kept and used for hunting. Miles refused to allow the Indians to keep any weapons, whereupon the talk ended. Before Joseph left the camp, Miles seized the chief and took him prisoner. The Indians retaliated, detaining Lieutenant Lovell H. Jerome until Miles released Joseph. General Howard reached the Bear Paw Mountains on October 4, but he did not assume command or direct the peace negotiations. Instead, Miles finished "the work he had so well begun."[73]

On October 5 two treaty Nez Perce negotiated a peace. *Meopkowit* (Old George) and *Jokais* (Captain John) served the army as scouts, and they rode into the Indian camp to tell the warriors that Miles and Howard wanted "no more war!"[74] This news provided the Indians an honorable way to end hostilities without surrendering. As

Yellow Wolf put it, "We were not captured. It was a draw battle."

The Indians understood that the army had agreed to a conditional surrender, whereby the warriors would not be punished but allowed to return to the reservation in Idaho. Joseph reported that Miles had said, "If you will come and give up your arms, I will spare your lives and send you back to the reservation." The Nez Perce and Palouse believed Miles or "they never would have surrendered."[75] Some of the Indians escaped to Canada, joining the Sioux under Sitting Bull. But most of the people--too old, tired, or sick to escape--surrendered. Husishusis Kute, now head of all Palouse, surrendered with the Nez Perce. Toward evening on the night of October 5, 1877, Joseph rode out to surrender. The chief rode forward with his rifle across the pommel of his saddle, and he halted his horse a few steps in front of Howard and Miles. Joseph dismounted, walked toward Howard and offered his rifle to the general. "Howard waved him to Miles. He then walked to Miles and handed him the rifle."[76] Joseph did not present the elegant speech so often attributed to him, but the chief was in fact sick and tired of fighting and greatly concerned about the sick and dying people who had fought with him. When he handed his rifle to Miles, he knew in his heart that he would never fight as a warrior again."

Over 400 Indians surrendered that cold October day at the Bear Paws, including Husishusis Kute and Palouse men, women, and children. The Palouse had suffered their last military defeat but not their final indignation. Like the Nez Perce, the Palouse anticipated their return to the Nez Perce Reservation. Instead, the soldiers sent them to Fort Keogh, Montana, before sending them on boats down the Yellowstone and Missouri Rivers. General William Tecumseh Sherman, commander of the United States army, ordered the Palouse and Nez Perce first sent to Fort Leavenworth, Kansas, and then to the Quapaw Agency in the Indian Territory.[77]

The Indians arrived at Fort Leavenworth on November 27, 1877, remaining there until July 21, 1878. Depression, death, and disease characterized their captivity at Fort Leavenworth, and during their eight months' stay, twenty-one and an unknown number of babies died., One observer reported the deplorable condition of the Palouse and Nez Perce at Fort Leavenworth. "The 400 miserable, helpless, emaciated specimens of humanity, subject for months to the malarial atmosphere of river bottoms, presented a picture which brought to my mind the horrors of Andersonville [a Civil War prison]." Over half of the Palouse and Nez Perce, "principally women and children," were sick, and all of the Indians suffered from the "poisonous maleria."[78]

The condition of the Palouse and Nez Perce at Fort Leavenworth was so dreadful that one individual stated that the Indians "had better be moved soon or their removal to the burial ground will be completed."[79]  In July, 1878, the soldiers moved the Palouse and Nez Perce to their new home on the Quapaw Agency in the Indian Territory.  They remained there for a year before the Bureau of Indian Affairs transferred them to the Ponca Agency in present-day north central Oklahoma near the town of Tonkawa.  The land upon which the Indians resettled had been chosen the previous October by Husishusis Kute and Joseph who found the lands located west of the Ponca Agency, near the junction of the Chikaskia and Salt Fort Rivers, more to their liking but unacceptable.[80]  At the Ponca Agency, the Palouse suffered the same problems as the Nez Perce.  They died of malnutrition, disease, and despair.

Indeed, starvation, sickness, and death characterized the entire exile of the Indians at *Eekish Pah*, the Hot Place.  Ponca Agent William H. Whiteman was ill-prepared to handle the Palouse and Nez Perce, and he candidly explained to the Indians that he "was utterly ignorant of the plans of the Department [of Indian Affairs]" to move them to his agency.  Consequently, the Indians received little food, clothing, shelter, or hope.  Worse yet, Whiteman had no quinine or medicine of any sort to combat disease, particularly malaria.[81]  The Indians made the best of the situation, and in the years following their removal to the Ponca Agency, they farmed, ranched, build homes, and attended mission schools. Yet, they held onto the hope that one day they would return to their beloved Northwest. During their years of exile the Indians looked to Husishusis Kute as their spiritual leader.[82] He led the people in singing, dancing, and praying in the old Washani faith, and through their tooat, the Indians asked for deliverance.

The Indian leaders--Husishusis Kute, Joseph, and Yellow Bull-- did not sit idly, praying for deliverance from a land described by Joseph as a "poor man; it amounts to nothing." The Indians fully cooperated with investigations by a Board of Indian Commissioners and Commissioner of Indian Affairs Ezra A. Hayt. The various investigations provided white interest in the Nez Perce situation, but the inquiries did little to boost the spirits of the Indians.[83] In January, 1879, Husishusis Kute, Joseph and Yellow Bull traveled to Washington, D.C., where they spoke to politicians and newspaper reporters who gave the Indians an enthusiastic reception. Joseph told them that his "heart was sad when I think of my home, which the Great Spirit gave my fathers."[84] The Indians met congressmen, senators, and the commissioner of Indian Affairs, but to no avail. Resentment against the Palouse and Nez Perce remained intense in the Northwest, and the government refused to permit the Indians to return to their homeland. Forever patient, the Indians did not give up hope.[85]

In March, 1879, Joseph returned to Washington, D.C., to plead his case, and once again, he received a grand reception. Joseph gave an interview to the popular *North American Review* which appeared in the April issue of the magazine under the title, "An Indian's View of Indians Affairs."[86] Joseph outlined the history of his people and explained his view of the Nez Perce problems, stating that he did "not believe that the Great Spirit Chief gave one kind of a man the right to tell another . . . what to do." According to his beliefs and those of the Indians he represented, "no man owned any part of the earth, and a man could not sell what he did not own." Joseph appealed to the American sense of democracy and equality: "All men were made by the Great Spirit Chief. They are all brothers. The earth is the mother of all people, and all people should have equal rights upon it." Chief Joseph expressed his opinions and his philosophy, and the essay won him personal acclaim while providing the Nez Perce and Palouse with nationwide recognition of their plight.[87]

Joseph's efforts provided few immediate results, however, and the Indians became increasingly sick in soul and body. When former Superintendent of Indian Affairs for Oregon A.B. Meacham visited the Indians in the fall of 1879, he reported that Chief Joseph said: "You come to see me as you would a man upon his death-bed. The Great Spirit above has left me and my people to our fate." Joseph believed that his people had been forgotten, saying that "death comes almost every day for some of my people. He will soon come for all of us." Joseph prophesied that the Palouse and Nez Perce were "a doomed people" who would soon "be in the ground."[88] As the Indians grew more depressed, the white community became more aware of the Nez Perce-Palouse situation.

As early as April, 1879, Indian Inspector John McNeil wrote to Commissioner Hayt stating that a "great wrong has been done this people." According to the inspector, "No other tribe moved to this territory has better claim to be returned to its homeland."[89] McNeil was not alone, as individuals and institutions petitioned congressmen and senators in support of the Indians. The pressure placed on the Indian bureau and the Congress resulted in a decision to return thirty-three women and children to the Nez Perce Reservation of Idaho. James Reuben, a Christian Nez Perce assigned to guide the first Indians back to their homeland, stated that words could not "express our joy when we remember that our feet will soon tread again our native land, and our eyes behold the scenes of our childhood. The undying love for home, which we have cherished in our hearts so long, has caused our tears to flow for years, but now we are but one step from that home, and how great is our joy."[90]

The public pressure on American Indian policy makers continued. Petitions, letters, and telegrams poured into Washington, D.C., from religious organizations, the Indian Rights Association, and congressmen and senators who championed the Nez Perce-Palouse cause. Women and women's organizations consistently supported the Indian cause through many diverse organizations. The entire movement gained impetus on Independence Day, 1884, when Senator Harry L. Dawes secured passage of a bill empowering the Secretary of Interior to decide the fate of the Indians. The Indians waited nearly a year, until April 29, 1885, when Commissioner of Indian Affairs John D. Atkins ordered the return of the Indians to the Northwest. The Commissioner assigned D. W. H. Faulkner special agent to oversee the transfer. Because of indictments against Joseph and others, the government divided the Indians into two groups. Agents appointed Husishusis Kute to accompany 118 people to the Nez Perce Reservation in Idaho, while Joseph and Yellow Bull took the remaining 150 Indians to the Colville Reservation in Washington. Of the original 431 Palouse and Nez Perce who arrived at Fort Leavenworth in 1877, only 268 left the Indian Territory on the morning of May 22, 1885.[91]

Before leaving the Indian Territory, Husishusis Kute, Joseph, and Yellow Bull willingly signed a document forfeiting their claim to any land in the territory. Tears of sorrow fell with tears of joy as the Indians boarded the train. Memories of their exile in the Hot Country filled their minds, as did their grief for the many children, the many loved ones they left behind. The Palouse and Nez Perce traveled together by rail until they reached Wallula Junction on the Columbia River, Washington Territory. Husishusis Kute took the Indians assigned to him to the Nez Perce Reservation, while Joseph and Yellow Bull traveled northward to the Colville Reservation.[92] Most Palouse went to the Colville Reservation with Joseph, but others settled on the Nez Perce Reservation with their friends and families. When Husishusis Kute arrived at Lapwai on May 27, he reported to Agent Monteith, but the Washani headman did not remain on the Nez Perce Reservation. Husishusis Kute joined Joseph and Yellow Bull on the Colville Reservation, living out his life among the Palouse and Nez Perce.

The Palouse who had fought and died with the Nez Perce returned to the Northwest with mixed feelings. They had fought as patriots, defending their homes, families, and beliefs, but they had been party to an ill-fated attempt to flee their homes and the grasp of the United States government. They had suffered severely, paying the ultimate price for their convictions. They had lost their children and they knew that the unborn would never know the free life on the Plateau, living along Snake River and riding the seasoned rounds of old. The Palouse returned to the Northwest worrying about their children and lamenting the immediate past. They returned to reservation life in the Northwest with an uncertain future but with a deep conviction to maintain that which was the heart of their community, their spiritual beliefs and their identity as Palouse Indians.

Snake River, site of Palouse villages.  Yakima Regional Library.

Palouse in front of mat lodge.  Yakima Regional Library.

Dr. Whirlwind. Oregon Historical Society.

He-Who-Watches, Palouse.  Bill Walter Collection.

William Craig, by Gustavus Sohon. Washington Historical Society.

Nez Perce entering the Walla Walla Council, 1855.  Smithsonian Institution.

Archie Lawyer, Mark Williams, James Reuben with Agent John Monteith.  Smithsonian  Institution.

Chief Joseph.  Yakima Regional Library.

General William Tecumseh Sherman.  Arizona Historical Society.

General Oliver O. Howard. National Archives.

Chief Lawyer by Gustavus Sohon. Washington State Historical Society.

Chief Timothy.  Yakima Regional Library.

Smohalla, Washani Prophet.  Yakima Regional Library.

Washani worship, Priest Rapids.  Yakima Regional Library.

Bones, Palouse.  Oregon Historical Society.

Yellow Hair, Palouse.  Yakima Regional Library.

Ollokot. Yakima Regional Library.

Ollokot.  Washington State University Library.

Peopeo Tahlikt, Bird Alighting.  Yakima Regional Library.

Hemene Moxmox, Yellow Wolf.  Washington State University Library.

Nez Perce Children.  University of Washington.

Warriors near Soap Lake.  Bob Eddy Collection.

Nez Perce-Palouse tipis on Colville Reservation.  Yakima Regional Library.

Hustul, Tom Hill, Nez Perce Warrior.  Smithsonian Institution.

Umatilla Jim, Charles Simpson, Willie Andrews. Yakima Regional Library.

# THE PALOUSE IN EEKISH PAH

## by Clifford E. Trafzer

In late autumn of 1980 Andrew George sat with three researchers at his daughter's home on the Yakima Reservation, telling them something of his life and of the history of his people. The white-haired elder sat at the kitchen table explaining how his parents and grandparents had told him scores of stories which he was instructed to learn and relearn with the passing of each winter. Andrew had to repeat these stories until he could retell them exactly as they had been taught to him! In this way he remembered stories relating to creation, the power of animals, the sacredness of the earth, and the importance of family relations.[93] For over three hours, Andrew spoke of many aspects of life and culture of the Palouse, Nez Perce, Yakima, and Spokane Indians of the Great Columbia Plain.

During the course of his discussions, Andrew outlined his family's geneaology, mentioning that his mother and her family had once lived in Oklahoma. "She never talked about it," Andrew said "because it was too painful." Andrew had learned this from his aunt, but this was all he knew about his mother's exile to the Indian Territory in the 1870's and 1880's. Several members of Andrew's family had been taken from Montana to the Indian Territory, including Andrew's grandfather, *Ipnamatwekin*, his grandmother, *Ananemart*, his great uncle, *Kutskuts Samyohut*, his aunt, *Saethayou*, and his own mother, *Ipnou Sietsanmy*. These were just a few of the Palouse Indians of the east central Washington Territory who had been forcefully removed to the Indian Territory as punishment for their participation in the Nez Perce War of 1877. Some Palouse Indians, particularly the Upper Palouse who lived in close proximity to the Nez Perce, had been drawn into the conflict in 1879. The lives of these Palouse Indians and the non-treaty Nez Perce were joined during the war. The Palouse and Nez Perce fought together throughout the Nez Perce War of 1877, and those who survived the bloodshed and removal ultimately shared a common exile in *Eekish Pah*, the Hot Place.[94]

During the nineteenth century the Palouse Indians were often identified as Nez Perce in historical documents and accounts dealing with the Inland Northwest. This was natural because both tribes shared a common language, culture, and religion. However, both maintained their own distinct dialect and tribal identity. By the 1850s whites began to recognize the subtle distinctions between the Palouse and Nez Perce, and by 1855, the government of the United States officially recognized their distinction by separating the two tribes during the Walla Walla Treaty Councils of May and June, 1855. The Nez Perce negotiated a separate treaty, while the Palouse were grouped with several other tribes and ordered onto the Yakima Reservation.[95]

Between 1855, when the treaties were signed, and the 1870s, when white settlements increased at an alarming rate, most Palouse remained on their land, refusing to remove to the reservations. Thus, in the face of miners, merchants, cattleman, and homesteaders, the Palouse stood firm in their resolve to remain on the land. However, in 1876, following the Battle of the Little Big Horn, white settlers throughout the Pacific Northwest demanded the forced removal of all non-reservation Indians onto the reserves. Both the United States Army and the Bureau of Indian Affairs urged the removal of the non-reservation Nez Perce of Oregon and Idaho. And to this end General Oliver O. Howard met with Chiefs Joseph, White Bird, Rainbow, and others to demand their removal to the Nez Perce Reservation of Idaho. In addition, General Howard and Nez Perce Agent John Monteith called for the removal of the Upper Palouse from the Snake River and the surrounding area in the Washington Territory.[96]

Howard and Monteith convened meetings with the Palouse and Nez Perce at Fort Lapwai in November, 1876 and in May 1877. At both meetings, Howard demanded the removal of the Indians to the reservation. The Indians pointed out that their forefathers had signed the first Nez Perce Treaty in 1855, which secured for them a large reservation containing most of their traditional homelands. Some of the Nez Perce had signed a subsequent treaty in 1863, which substantially reduced the reservation to one tenth of its former size. Many Nez Perce refused to abide by the so-called "Thief Treaty" and were labeled the non-treaty faction of the tribe. The Palouse were not included in this treaty, but because of their residence so near the Nez Perce Reservation, they too were told to remove. When Howard and Monteith convened their second Lapwai Council in 1877, some representatives of the Palouse were present to listen and participate. Indeed, Husishusis Kute, a headman and religious leaders of a traditional Indian faith known as the Washani, was selected by all of the Indians to speak after the eldest spiritual leader, a Nez Perce named Toohoolhoolzote.[97]

The deliberations at the Lapwai Council of 1877 did not go well for the Indians, and Husishusis Kute never had an opportunity to speak. An ugly quarrel developed soon after the proceedings began between Toohoolhoolzote and Howard over the "chieftainship" of the earth and the inability of the Indians to surrender lands that had been entrusted to them by God. "You white people get together, measure the earth, and then divide it."   Pointing out that only a portion of the tribe had agreed to the Thief Treaty, Toohoolhoolzote stated that "Part of the Indians gave up their land. I never did. The earth is part of my body, and I never gave up the earth."[98]

The Palouse and Nez Perce were in agreement on these points. It was literally against their religion to divide the earth into parcels, since the earth was the giver and sustainer of all life. According to their spiritual beliefs, God was the creator and the earth the mother of all life. To tamper with the earth--to plow, mine, or sub-divide the land--was against God's law. Toohoolhoolzote warned Howard that the general was in danger of committing a grave sin: "You are trifling with the law of the earth."[99]   Hostility broke out when Toohoolhoolzote continued his line of reasoning, refusing to agree to move to the reservation. He was seized by soldiers and jailed. For a few minutes, the Palouse and Nez Perce waivered indecisively between war and peace, but they ultimately decided to move to the Nez Perce Reservation to avoid war. The elders prevailed that day, for they knew that they could not win a war against the suyapo, the white men.[100]

The two major Palouse leaders, Husishusis Kute and Hahtalekin, returned to the Snake River to gather their people, property, and animals for their short journey to the reservation. Hahtalekin was resigned to the removal, but Husishusis Kute and his emissaries traveled far and wide to rally militant support for the non-treaty Indians.[101]   Husishusis Kute failed in his mission, but both he and Hahtalekin joined the Nez Perce after open warfare erupted on June 12, 1877 when blood was shed and war was triggered by three young Nez Perce.   Although some Palouse were likely present during the subsequent Battle of White Bird Canyon and the fights near the Salmon River, most Palouse joined the war after the Clearwater Battle in north-central Idaho.[102]   The Palouse fought with the Nez Perce in all the major battles in Idaho and Montana, including the Battle of the Big Hole where Hahtalekin and his son Pahka Pahtahank (Five Fogs) were killed in the fierce fighting.[103]   From the Big Hole through the Yellowstone National Park, and from Canyon Creek to the Bear Paw Mountains, Palouse men, women, and children fought for their freedom until their total surrender on October 5, 1877.[104]

Before the fighting ended, Chief Joseph negotiated an honorable surrender on behalf of the Nez Perce and Palouse.   The Indians believed that they would spend the winter of 1877 at Fort Keogh in Montana and be returned to the Nez Perce Reservation the following spring.   This is what they had understood from their negotiations with Colonel Nelson A. Miles and General Howard.   But when news of the surrender reached William Tecumseh Sherman, the General of the United States Army, he revised this decision and ordered the Indians to be punished by sending them to the Indian Territory. Sherman argued that the Nez Perce and Palouse "must never be allowed to return to Oregon, but should be engrafted on the Modoc in [the] Indian country."

From Chicago, the headquarters of the Missouri Division of the Army, General Philip Sheridan ordered the Nez Perce and Palouse to be sent to Fort Leavenworth, Kansas. There the Palouse and Nez Perce were to be held as prisoners of war until the Bureau of Indian Affairs found a suitable site for the Indians, preferably in the Indian Territory. Soon after, General Howard concurred with Sherman and Sheridan, calling for the removal of these Northwestern Indians from their homelands. Only Colonel Miles remained committed to his agreement that the Indians should be returned to Idaho, but Miles had no power to reverse the decision of Sherman and Sheridan. The Indians were to be removed and they were ultimately to be located in present-day Oklahoma.[105]

In November, 1877, Sherman ordered Miles to take his prisoners down the Yellowstone and Missouri Rivers to Fort Lincoln near Bismark, North Dakota. Of the 431 Indians who were escorted downstream, only a minority were Palouse. Their exact numbers are unknown due to the fact that the army never distinguished between the Nez Perce and Palouse. Still, some of the prisoners were Palouse

Indians, including Husishusis Kute who was considered a prominent headman along with Joseph and Yellow Bull. The Indians all shared the same fate, leaders and followers, Palouse and Nez Perce. They all made their way downstream to St. Paul, Minnesota, and by train were shipped to Fort Leavenworth, Kansas.

The Indians were settled on a horrible site "about two miles above the fort, between a lagoon and the [Missouri] River, the worst possible place that could have been selected." The condition of the people, already deplorable from the effects of the war and the long journey, became even worse. The Indians were described as "miserable, helpless, emaciated specimens of humanity." Half of the people particularly women and children, were sick and dying. Their condition worsened the following spring and summer, and by July, 1879 "at least 21 Nez Perce [and possibly Palouse] had died of sickness in the pesthole." The death toll was probably higher because the army did not record the number of babies lost or those who died during childbirth.[106]

The Palouse and Nez Perce remained at Fort Leavenworth until July 19, 1878 when the government ordered the Indians removed to the Quapaw Reserve in the Indian Territory. General Sherman had never intended for them to remain at the fort, since he wanted the Indian Bureau to assume responsibility over them. Under the provisions of the Indian Appropriation Act of May 27, 1878 the Palouse and Nez Perce were instructed to move to the extreme northeaster corner of present-day Oklahoma where they would live near another exiled tribe from the Northwest, the Modocs. Congress appropriated twenty thousand dollars for the removal of the Palouse and Nez Perce and for food, clothing, and "other articles...required for their advancement in civilization."[107]   With the congressional allocation, the Bureau of Indian Affairs took control of the Palouse and Nez Perce, loaded them on railroad cars, and shipped them to Baxter Springs, Kansas, the headquarters of the Quapaw Agency.   Over two hundred Indians were ill before the journey, and many people were bedridden because of disease and heat exhaustion.   Three children died during the trip.[108]

The Indians arrived at Baxter Springs on July 21 and spent the night at the agency headquarters before moving the next day to their new home.   By wagons, the Palouse and Nez Perce traveled seven miles into the Indian Territory where they were greeted by friendly Modocs who offered presents of potatoes, beans, and corn.   A welcoming feast was arranged by the Modocs, and likely some Senecas, Wyandots, Peorias, Miamis, Quapaws, Ottowas, Shawnees, and others living on the same reservation attended this gathering.

The reception received by the Palouse and Nez Perce was not equalled by the Quaker Agent, Hiram W. Jones, who was not prepared to receive the new arrivals. In late summer, when driving rains drenched the region, the Indians were without shelter or dry fuel for fires. Without horses, and facing the rising streams, the Indians were unable to reach Baxter Springs to retrieve their baggage and much-needed quinine. They shifted for themselves and watched their people die from pneumonia, influenza, malaria, and depression. By October, 1878, another 47 people had perished and the future of the Palouse and Nez Perce in *Eekish Pah* did not seem promising.[109]

In order to investigate first hand the condition of the Palouse and Nez Perce, Commissioner of Indian Affairs E.A. Hayt and a board of commissioners visited the Quapaw Agency in October, 1878. Hayt heard Chief Joseph's arguments that the Indians had agreed to a conditional surrender, whereby they were to be sent to Idaho, not the Indian Territory. The Commissioner told Joseph that the people could not be returned to the Northwest, but that he would help them find a better home in the Indian Territory. Hayt reported that he took "Joseph with his interpreter [Arthur Chapman] and Chief Husishusis Kute (Bald Head), with me about 250 miles."

The Commissioner traveled with Husishusis Kute and Joseph for over a week, riding through portions of Kansas and the Indian

Territory. Hayt found both chiefs to be the "most gentlemenly and well-behaved Indians I ever met." The Commissioner and the Indians ultimately reached the Ponco Agency near present-day Tonkawa, Oklahoma, where Husishusis Kute and Joseph agreed to move. Their new home was situated on lands consisted of 90,710 acres near the junction of the Salt Fork of the Arkansas and the Chicaskia Rivers. The land was fertile and some was well timbered. While visiting the Ponca Reservation, Husishusis Kute and Joseph met Chief White Eagle of the Poncas and twenty other headmen of the same tribe.

The meeting between the Indians was most cordial, but the following morning the Palouse and Nez Perce chiefs returned to the Quapaw Agency. Joseph had compared land on the Quapaw Agency to a poor man saying that the land "amounts to nothing."[110] And neither Joseph nor Husishusis Kute were enamored with the prospect of moving to another site in the Indian Territory. Both chiefs held to their resolve that they should be returned to the Nez Perce Reservation in Idaho. Although the prospects seemed remote, the Indians prayed for their return home. Indeed, while Joseph assumed the responsibility of dealing with whites in order to bring about the return of the people to the Northwest, Husishusis Kute led the people in prayers, songs, and dances designed to bring about the same end, but through different means.

Husishusis Kute returned to the Quapaw Agency and told the people--Palouse and Nez Perce--of his journey and the council with the Poncas. Furthermore, Husishusis Kute, the most important religious leader among the exiled Palouse and Nez Perce, prayed for the return of the people to the Northwest. Even after his removal to the Indian Territory, Husishusis Kute continued to worship in accordance with the precepts of the Washani faith. This religion was non-violent, but it demanded strict adherence to cultural and social ways that are distinctly Indian. Husishusis Kute and others taught that the Indians should ward off all things that were white and grew on the earth.

Through formal ceremonies, usually conducted on Sundays, Husishusis Kute offered the people spiritual hope and guidance during a tragic period.[111] While Husishusis Kute and his followers sang, prayed, and danced in an appeal to God for help, Joseph and Yellow Bull traveled to Washington, D.C., to appeal their case to the political leaders of the United States. The two Nez Perce were well received in Washington, particularly Joseph who fit the white man's image of a charismatic Indian orator, but the *Washington Post* and *Evening Star* made him bigger than life in their articles on the plight of the Nez Perce. On January 14 Joseph addressed many important leaders, and he stimulated a great deal of interest in the Nez Perce cause. Yet, he returned to the Quapaw Agency knowing that for the time being he would not be allowed to return to his beloved homeland.[112]

When Joseph and Yellow Bull returned to the Quapaw Agency, they found that preparations were being made for the removal of the people to the Ponca Reserve. Removal was delayed until parties of white and Cherokees settlers could be dissuaded from establishing residence on lands designated for the Palouse and Nez Perce. Finally, on June 6, 1879, the Indians began their 177 miles journey to their new home. By wagon train, and with Arthur Chapman acting as wagon master, the Indian emigrants traveled along the southern border of Kansas through such towns as Coffeyville, Peru, and Arkansas City.[113] Special Agent J.M. Haworth, who headed the removal, left the Palouse and Nez Perce at the mouth of the Chikaskia River and informed William Whiteman that the Indians were a part of the Ponca Agency.

Whiteman was totally unprepared for the Indians. He had received no prior word that they were coming; he had no food or shelter for them; and he had no quinine whatsoever for the Poncas, Palouse, or Nez Perce. Since the people arrived in mid-June, it was too late to plant, so Whiteman therefore put the Palouse and Nez Perce to work cutting native grasses for hay. The Indians also turned the sod of over two hundred acres of ground in preparation for the spring planting. Some of the Indians submitted to the labor, while others refused to work. Whiteman wrote that "Hard work has nothing to fear from them, they will handle it very gently." And one visitor, former Superintendent of Indian Affairs for Oregon Andrew B. Meachem, complained that the Indians were under the influence of a traditional spiritual leader who preached that it was against God's law to till the soil or to submit to white ways. The "medicine man" was Husishusis Kute who preached and practiced the traditional precepts of the Washani faith. The teachings of Husishusis Kute were contrary to government policy and contained elements of Indian life which the government hoped to eradicate.[114]

To counter the religious influence of the Washani, Hayt, Whitemen, and other agents encouraged the spread of Christianity among the Indians. As early as 1878, three young Christian Nez Perce missionaries were sent from Idaho to the Indian Territory to proselytize the non-Christian Nez Perce and Palouse. Mark Williams, Archie Lawyer, and James Reuben missionized their brothers, offering them the "white man's road." Williams and Lawyer returned to the Northwest shortly after their arrival in the Indian Territory, but Reuben remained until 1883.[115] The government's attempt to Christianize and "civilize" the Indians met with little success, despite the trials suffered during their exile in the Indian Territory.

The Palouse and Nez Perce faced many adversaries after their arrival, and chief among them was disease. Malaria continually plagued the people as did other diseases, including heart and lung ailments. Of the 431 people who had arrived in Fort Leavenworth in 1878, only 287 had survived by 1884. Many had died of disease, while others perished from the lack of food and shelter. The Indians did not sit idly and watch each other perish. Some lived off of their rations, but many engaged in such enterprises as gardening, freighting, and herding. Indeed, most of the Indians made a concerted effort to supplement their income by raising wheat, corn, and other vegetables.[116]

During the first year the Nez Perce and Palouse lived at the Ponca Agency little progress was made in the way of agriculture. The next year, 1881, was no better, despite the fact that the Indians had tilled, planted, and nurtured the crops. The corn and wheat, crops cultivated as a collective effort, failed miserably, and individual vegetable gardens fared even worse.[117] Not deterred by this failure, the Indians replanted the next spring. The spring and summer of 1882 were mild and the rains sufficient to produce a bountiful yield of corn, wheat, and hay.[118]

The fall of 1883 witnessed additional bumper crops of potatoes, melons, corn, and wheat. According to Lewellyn E. Woodin, the new agent, Chief Joseph and his wife produced 150 melons, 150 bushels of wheat, and 50 chickens.[119] The horn of plenty that had blessed the Palouse and Nez Perce the two previous years was hollow following the fall harvest of 1884. A drought swept the Great Plains, and crops everywhere wilted from lack of water, hot winds, and scorching sun. The Nez Perce and Palouse families harvested some corn and wheat, but personal gardens burned up entirely.[120] It was fortunate for the Indians that Husishusis Kute, Joseph, and Yellow Bull had signed a grazing lease in February, whereby the people would receive $2,000 for leasing 75,000 acres on the Oakland Reserve. Yet the money earned from grazing leases did little to relieve the food shortage and the severe depression suffered by Indians who lamented their exile and longed for the mountains, plateaus, and rivers of their former homes.[121]

While many Indians lost hope and slipped into the depths of despair, others did their utmost to have the people returned to the Northwest. Within the Indian community, no one was more instrumental in presenting the Nez Perce-Palouse cause than Chief Joseph. The Nez Perce leader had traveled to Washington, D.C., in January and March of 1879 to plead the case of the exiles. On his visits, Joseph stirred the conscience of many white Americans by his straightforward remarks.

Joseph granted an interview to the popular magazine, the *North American Review*, in which he set forth the Indian view of the Nez Perce War, their exile to the Indian Territory, and government Indian policies. "You might as well expect the rivers to run backward as that any man who was born free should be contented penned up and denied liberty to go where he pleases." Joseph asked for one law for all people and equal treatment under the law. "Treat all men alike. Give them all the same law. Give them all an even chance to live and grow. All men were made by the Great Spirit Chief. They are all brothers. The earth is the mother of all people, and all people should have equal rights upon it." Joseph's appeal was far reaching, and scores of people took up the Nez Perce cause. The chief met President Rutherford B. Hayes, Secretary of Interior Carl Schurz, Commissioner of Indian Affairs E.A. Hayt, and other prominent politicians, appealing to them all to honor the terms of the conditional surrender at the Bear Paws.[122]

Among the nation's politicians, Joseph's appeals fell on deaf ears, but other elements of the white population began an effort which ultimately led to the return of the Nez Perce and Palouse to the Northwest. The Indian Rights Association, the Presbyterian church, and even the wife of President James A. Garfield lobbied on behalf of the Indians. From every corner of the nation petitions, protests, and memorials flooded into the Congress and the White House and brought pressure to bear on the country's policy makers.[123] Additional pressure also likely came from cattlemen who coveted the grazing land occupied by the Palouse and Nez Perce in the Indian Territory.[124]

A large amount of publicity was generated in newspapers and magazines regarding the plight of the Indians, until all of this pressure finally bore fruit. In 1883 James Reuben returned to the Nez Perce Reservation with thirty-three widows and orphaned children. When Reuben learned of the decision, he recorded that words "cannot express our joy when we remember that our feet will soon tread again [on] our native land, and our eyes beyond the scenes of our childhood."[125] A year after Reuben returned to Idaho, a congres-sional act was passed on July 4, 1884 which authorized the Secretary of Interior to determine the fate of the Nez Perce and Palouse.

When word reached the Indians that their removal seemed imminent, they celebrated with a major feast. However, their removal to the Northwest was delayed by the Interior Department, in part because in 1878 thirty-one Nez Perce had been indicted for murder in the First District Court of Idaho. The Interior Department feared that the Territory of Idaho would pursue the case, particularly against Joseph. Government agents met with Joseph, Husishusis Kute, Yellow Bull, and others to explain the delay and the problem of returning all of them to Idaho. To prevent problems, the government proposed to divide the people, returning some to Washington and some to Idaho. This proposal did not impress the Indians, all of whom wanted to remain together. As a result of these complications, the Indians waited another nine months before preparations were made for their return home.[126]

On April 29, 1885 the Commissioner of Indian Affairs appointed W.H. Faulkner special agent to the Nez Perce and Palouse. Faulkner met with the Indian leaders, helped them to dispose of their property, and divided them into two groups. Joseph, Yellow Bull, Yellow Bear, and Husishusis Kute acted on behalf of the people and signed away their ownership to over 90,000 acres in the Indian Territory. In return, the Bureau of Indian Affairs agreed to pay for the return of the people to the Northwest. The Palouse and Nez Perce wept with joy when they learned of their return, and they wept at the thought of leaving the graves of so many loved ones in the heart of the Indian Territory.

At daybreak on May 21, 1885, 34 wagons, overloaded with the aged, the infirm, and the personal baggage, moved out from the Ponca Reserve. After nearly seven years of exile, the Nez Perce and Palouse began their long journey home. Throughout the day most of the people walked through the rain-soaked red mud until they reached a point on the railroad ten miles from Arkansas City. By 1:15 pm the next day all of the people and their belongings had been loaded on the Atchison, Topeka, and Santa Fe Railroad. At McPherson, Kansas, the Indians were transferred to the Union Pacific Railroad which carried the people through Denver, Cheyenne, and Pocatello. With a company of soldiers as an escort, the Indians traveled to Wallula, Washington. Without injury to person or property, the Palouse and Nez Perce had returned to the Pacific Northwest.[127]

At Wallula junction the Indians were split into two groups. Some Palouse were a part of the 118 Indians who were taken to the Nez Perce Reservation in Idaho. These Indians--composed of followers of Christianity and the Washani--were placed under the care of the Palouse religious leader, Husishusis Kute. Other Palouse remained with Joseph and Yellow Bull, and were among the 148 Indians transferred to the Colville Reservation in north-central Washington Territory. Thus, like the Nez Perce, the Palouse people were divided as a result of decisions made outside their control. Some of them were to remain on the Colville Reservation where their heirs reside today.

Not all of the Indians who moved to Idaho were Christians, for some of them adhered to the old Washani faith. But pressure was brought to bear on the Washani followers to convert to Christianity.

The schism between Christian and Washani Indians had long been a source of trouble among the Indians of the Inland Northwest. The arrival of so many non-Christians at Fort Lapwai complicated the issue and created even deeper factions. These divisions remained throughout the nineteenth century, and some have persisted to this day.[128]

Eventually, some of the Indians who first chose to live on the Nez Perce Reservation, including Husishusis Kute, moved to the Colville Reservation to reside with Chief Joseph's band near the agency headquarters of Nespelem. Husishusis Kute, Joseph, and Yellow Bull all lived out their lives on the Colville Reservation and are buried in sandy, wind-swept cemetaries in Nespelem. Other Palouse and Nez Perce who had once lived in the Indian Territory are buried in Idaho. This includes the grandfather, grandmother, aunt and uncle of Andrew George. But at least two members of Andrew's family--an uncle and a grandmother--died in the Indian Territory and are buried in Oklahoma. Andrew George and many other Palouse and Nez Perce Indians share a common heritage of life and toil with the Indian people of Oklahoma. More specifically, the Palouse and Nez Perce share a common tie with the people of the Quapaw and Ponca Reserves where so many dead now lay. For the Palouse, their exile in Eekish Pah, the Hot Place, was not a pleasant one. Indeed, their experience in Eekish Pah was perhaps best expressed in a book by the Nez Perce Tribe: "Our Oklahoma exile was a time of sadness and sorrow."[129]

# ENDNOTES

[1] *Indians and the Invasion of the Inland Pacific Northwest* and is published here with the permission of Washington State University Press, Pullman, Washington. Ralph Burcham, ed., "Orofino Gold," *Idaho Yesterday* 4 (1960); 2-9; Hubert Howe Bancroft, *History of Washington, Idaho, and Montana*, pp. 234-35; Josephy, *The Nez Perce Indian*, (New Haven, 1965), pp. 691-95. For a new study of the Nez Perce, see Clifford E. Trafzer, *The Nez Perce* (New York: Chelsea House, 1992).

[2] McWhorter. *Hear Me*, p. 99. After the war in 1858, George Wright was promoted to general. His recommendation to Superintendent Geary to permit miners to dig for gold on the Nez Perce Reservation was an abridgement of assurances the general had made to his Nez Perce scouts during the war in 1858.

[3] Ibid.; Josephy, *The Nez Perce*, pp. 412-14.

[4] Josephy, *The Nez Perce*, pp. 421-22.

[5] Ibid., pp. 423-26; McWhorter, *Hear Me*, pp. 106-107. For details of the agreement of the money paid the Nez Perce, see Josephy, *The Nez Perce.* p. 429.

[6] Joseph, "An Indian's View of Indian Affairs," pp. 412-33; hereafter all entries are cited from the same article published in Cyrus T. Brady, *Northwestern Fights and Fighters*. Joseph stated that "In the treaty councils the commissioners have claimed that our country had been sold to the Government. Suppose a white man should come to me and say, 'Joseph, I like your horses, and I want to buy them' I say to him, 'No, my horses suit me, I will not sell them'. Then he goes to my neighbor and says to him: 'Joseph has some good horses. I want to buy them but he refuses to sell'. My neighbor answers, 'Pay me the money, and I will sell you Joseph's horses'. The white man returns to me and says,

'Joseph, I have bought your horses, and you must let me have them'. If we sold our lands to the Government, this is the way they were bought."

[7] Oral interview by authors with Mary Jim, November 9,10, 1979.

[8] Monteith to J.Q. Smith, March 19, 1877 in Josephy, *The Nez Perce*, p. 493. "Report of Civil and Military Commission to Nez Perce Indians, Washington Territory and Northwest, *Annual Report of the Secretary of Interior*, 1877, pp. 607-609. For the best published source on Smohalla, see Click Relander, *Drummers and Dreamers* (Caldwell, Id.: Caxton Printers Ltd., 1956). Margery B. Sharkey has authored a fine essay on Smohalla entitled, "The Wanapums and the Priest Rapids Dam: Fulfillment of an Indian Prophecy," which will be published by the *Pacific Northwest Quarterly;* see also Chapter 7 of James Mooney, "The Ghost Dance Religion," *Fourteenth Annual Report of the Bureau of Ethnology* (Washington, D.C., 1986).

[9] "Report of...Commission to Nez Perce Indians," *Annual Report of the Secretary of Interior*, 1877, pp. 607-609.

[10] Ibid.; Oliver O. Howard, *Nez Perce Joseph* (Boston, 1881), p. 30.

[11] Josephy, *The Nez Perce*, pp. 489-90.

[12] "Report of...Commission to Nez Perce Indians," *Annual Report of the Secretary of Interior*, pp. 607-609.

[13] Ibid.

[14] Ibid.

[15] *Annual Report of the Secretary of War* 1, 1877, pp. 115-16; hereafter cited as *Annual Report, SW*. Also, see Chester A. Fee, *Chief Joseph* (New York, 1936), p. 97.

[16] *Annual Report of the Secretary of War* (SW) 1, 1877, pp. 587-90; Howard, *Nez Perce Joseph*, pp. 37, 43. On March 14, 1877 Howard ordered two companies of cavalry armed

with two Gatling Guns to prepare for action. He then ordered his soldiers to occupy the confluence of the Wallowa and Grande Ronde Rivers. When the soldiers arrived, Ollokot visited Monteith and requested another council with government officials which was forwarded to the Commissioner of Indian Affairs. A similar request reached the ears of Howard who agreed to meet with Ollokot on April 20, 1877. Ollokot and Howard parlayed at Fort Walla Walla where they agreed to hold another council. The Palouse and Nez Perce were then summoned to the second Lapwai Council.

[17]Howard, *Nez Perce Joseph,* p. 54.

[18] Ibid., p. 63; McWhorter, *Hear Me,* pp. 171.

[19] McWhorter Collection, Manuscripts and Archives, WSU, Folder 213, B/70; McWhorter, *Hear Me,* pp. 172-73.

[20] McWhorter Collection, Manuscripts and Archives, WSU, Folder 213, B/37; McWhorter, *Hear Me,* pp. 172-73.

[21] McWhorter, *Hear Me,* p. 172.

[22] Ibid.

[23] McWhorter Collection, Manuscripts and Archives, WSU, Folder, 213, B/37.

[24] Ibid., and Folder 213, b/70.

[25] Howard, *Nez Perce Joseph,* pp. 58-64. Toohoolhoolzote told Howard: "You have no right to compare us, grown men, to children. Children do not think for themselves. Grown men do think for themselves." Toohoolhoolzote concluded that the government in Washington, D.C., could not speak for the Indians, but Howard quickly refuted his assertions.

[26] Ibid., pp. 64-66.

[27] Joseph, "An Indian's View of Indian Affairs," p. 57.

[28] Howard, *Nez Perce Joseph*, p. 69.

[29] McWhorter Collection, Manuscripts and Archives, WSU, Folder 213, B/70.

[30] Howard, *Nez Perce Joseph*, p. 71; McWhorter, *Hear Me*, pp. 184-185.

[31] Joseph, "An Indian's View of Indian Affairs," p. 19.

[32] McWhorter Collection, Manuscripts and Archives, WSU, Folder 213, B/69.

[33] Howard, *Nez Perce Joseph*, p. 72.

[34] Oral interview by authors with Mary Jim, November 9, 10, 1979.

[35] McWhorter, *Yellow Wolf*, p. 42: Josephy, *The Nez Perce*, p. 511.

[36] Oral interview by authors with Mary Jim, November 9, 10, 1979 and April 25, 1980.

[37] Oliver O. Howard, *My Life and Experiences among Our Hostile Indians* (Hartford, Conn., 1907), pp. 262-64.

[38] Ibid., pp. 271-79.

[39] *New Northwest*, June 21, 1878; McWhorter, *Hear Me*, pp. 195-96. An excellent study of the beginning stages of the Nez Perce War is John D. McDermott, *Forlorn Hope: The Battle of White Bird Canyon and the Beginning of the Nez Perce War* (Boise, 1978), pp. 3-12. The first raid on the Salmon River occurred on June 13, 1877.

[40] Robert I. Burns, *The Jesuits and the Indian Wars* (New Haven, 1966), p. 392.

[41] Davenport Letter, *Walla Walla Watchman*, June 22, 1877.

42 *Lewiston Tribune*, June 23, 1877.

43 *Walla Walla Watchman*, June 22, 1877; W.H. Lever, *History of Whitman County*, (N.P., 1901), pp. 235-36; George Sutherland, "A Half Century in Eastern Washington," unpublished manuscript, Oliphant Collection, Manuscripts and Archives, WSU.

44 *Lewiston Teller*, June 24, 1877.

45 *Walla Walla Watchman*, June 23, 1877; *Walla Walla Union*, June 23, 1877; and Lever, *History of Whitman County*, pp. 235-36.

46 *Walla Walla Watchman*, June 21, 1877; Lever, *History of Whitman County*, pp. 359, 411; John D. Butler, "Reminiscences of an Old Timer," Oliphant Collection, Manuscripts and Archives, WSU.

47 *Lewiston Teller*, June 24, 1877; *Walla Walla Union*, June 23, 1877; and *Walla Walla Watchman*, June 29, 1877; oral interview by authors with Leonard Jones, July 16, 1980.

48 D.S. Bowman's story is found in Lever, *History of Whitman County*, pp. 235-36.

49 *Walla Walla Union*, June 25, 1877; Burns, *The Jesuits and the Indian Wars*, p. 385.

50 Joset to Simms, July 4, 1877 and Joseph Giorda, "Blessing in Disguise," in Joset and Giorda Collections, Oregon Province Archives of the Society of Jesus, Gonzaga University, Spokane, Washington; hereafter cited as O.J.

51 Ibid.; Spalgalt to Howard, June 21, 1877, Giorda Collection, OJ; McWhorter, *Yellow Wolf*, p. 36 and McWhorter, *Hear Me*, pp. 171-73.

52 *Walla Walla Union*, June 23, 1877.

53 Joset Diary, June 23, 1877, Joset Collection, OJ.

[54] Burns, *The Jesuits and the Indian Wars*, p. 396; Giorda, "Blessing in Disguise," Giorda Collection, OJ.

[55] *Walla Walla Union*, June 23, 1877.

[56] Giorda, "Blessing in Disguise," Giorda Collection, OJ. This manuscript contains a valuable letter from Chief Seltice.

[57] *Lewiston Teller*, June 27, 1877; Burns, *The Jesuits and the Indian Wars*, p. 397.

[58] Ewart to Joset, June 27, 1877, Joset Collection, OJ.

[59] Crowley to Ewart and Davenport in Frank T. Gilbert, *Historic Sketches* (Portland, Or., 1882), pp. 436-37.

[60] McWhorter, *Yellow Wolf*, p. 63. McWhorter provided this discussion of Kosooyeen on the same page in *Yellow Wolf*: "This intrepid young man's prewar name was Wewass Pahkalatkeikt (Five Sun-Rayed Bile). It is contended by some Nez Perce that the proper spelling is Kosooyoom, but since Yellow Wolf and other contemporaries pronounced the name as first spelled, that form will be used. Kosooyeen was reputed by his compatriots to be a brave warrior and adroit scout. A fine-looking young man, he resembled in many respects Chief Ollokot; both were general favorites with the people. He belonged to Chief Hahtalekin's Paloos, but was more often with Chief Joseph's band, because of his sister's marriage to one of its members. At the last battle Kosooyeen escaped to join Sitting Bull, but, returning with other refugees, he was arrested at Pendleton, Oregon, and banished to Indian Territory. He died on the Nez Perce Reservation in the early thirties. The writer knew him only as Luke Andrews."

[61] McDermott, *Forlorn Hope*, p. 34; McWhorter, *Yellow Wolf*, pp. 48-49 and McWhorter, *Hear Me*, p. 224. The fact that some Upper Palouse were related to Looking Glass and others is verified by several Palouse and Nez Perce elders, particularly Mrs. M. Lawyer who is the most informed individual on the Nez Perce Reservation today regarding genealogies of tribal families.

[62] No attempt is made here to narrate the details of the Nez Perce War of 1877. Entire volumes have been written detailing the conflict. For the best volumes on the war, see Mark H. Brown, *Flight of the Nez Perce* (New York, 1967); Josephy, *The Nez Perce*; McDermott, *Forlorn Hope*; Fee, *Chief Joseph*; Howard, *Nez Perce Joseph*; McWhorter, *Hear Me*; McWhorter, *Yellow Wolf*; Bancroft, *History of Washington, Idaho, and Montana*; and Beal *"I Will Fight No More Forever."*

[63] Peter Ronan, *Historical Sketches of the Flathead Indian Nation* (Helena, Mont., 1890), pp. 64-66; McWhorter, *Hear Me*, pp. 347-54; McWhorter, *Yellow Wolf*, p. 107; *New Northwest*, December 27, 1878. The only trouble encountered by the Palouses and the Nez Perce occurred at the eastern end of the Lolo Trail at Fort Missoula, Montana. There the Indians met a few troops under Captain Charles C. Rawn, but no conflict developed after the Indians agreed to ride through the Bitterroot Valley without disturbing the white settlers or their property. Because Rawn refused to engage the Indians or to impede their escape, his post was nicknamed "Fort Fizzle."

[64] Josephy, *The Nez Perce*, pp. 563-72, 77-78; McWhorter, *Hear Me*, p. 369.

[65] Gibbon's Report, *Annual Report, SW* 1, 1876-1877, pp. 501-505; also see Gibbon's "The Battle of the Big Hole," *Harper's Weekly* 39 (1895): 1215-16 and 1235-36; McWhorter, *Yellow Wolf*, p. 112; G.O. Shields, "The Battle of the Big Hole," in Brady, *Northwestern Fights and Fighters*, pp. 164-90.

[66] Peopeo Tholek to McWhorter, July, 1928 in McWhorter, *Hear Me*, p. 380.

[67] See Wounded Head's Narrative and Young White Bird's Story in McWhorter, *Hear Me*, pp. 372-76.

[68] McWhorter, *Yellow Wolf*, p. 119.

[69] Ibid.

[70] Beal, "I Will Fight No More Forever," pp. 161-229'; Brown, *Flight of the Nez Perce*, chapters 16-20; *New Northwest*, August 24, September 14, October 12, 1877; Charles E.S.

Wood, "An Indian Epic is Re-told," *The Spectator*, September 14, 1929; McWhorter, *Yellow Wolf*, pp. 162-218; Howard, *Nez Perce Joseph*, pp. 226-69; McWhorter, *Hear Me*, pp. 404-77; Josephy, *The Nez Perce*, pp. 590-612; Narrative of Peopeo Tholekt, McWhorter Collection, Manuscripts and Archives, WSU.

[71] McWhorter, *Yellow Wolf*, pp. 187-205; McWhorter, *Hear Me*, pp. 478-82; Henry Romlyn, "The Capture of Chief Joseph and His Nez Perce Indians", *Contributions of the Historical Society of Montana* 2 (1896); 286; Josephy, pp. 612-18; Brown, *Flight of the Nez Perces*, chapters 22-25.

[72] McWhorter, *Hear Me*, pp. 480-90; Josephy, *The Nez Perce*, pp. 619-25; McWhorter, *Yellow Wolf*, pp. 214-17; Charles E.S. Wood, "The Pursuit and Caoture of Chief Joseph," in Fee, *Chief Joseph*, pp. 324-26. Primary sources on the meeting between Joseph and Miles include Affadavit of Tom Hill, "Memorial of the Nez Perce Indians, Residing in the State of Idaho to the Congress of the United States," Senate *Executive Document 97*, 62nd Cong., 1st Sess., SS 6108; Lovell Jerome, "Indian Battle Retold," *The Otsego Journal*, July 17, 1930; Miles' Report, December 27, 1877, *Annual Report, SW* 1, 1876-1877, p. 629; and Miles, *Personal Recollections and Observations*, p. 276.

[73] Howard;s Report, December 27, 1877, *Annual Report SW* 1, 1876-877, pp. 630-31.

[74] McWhorter, *Yellow Wolf*, p. 224.

[75] Ibid., p. 225; Joseph, "An Indian's View of Indian Affairs", p. 429.

[76] Wood, "An Indian EPIC," *The Spectator;* Wood to McWhorter, January 31, 1936, McWhorter Collection, WSU, Folder 181.

[77] The number of Indians who surrendered at the Bear Paws varies, but 431 arrived at Fort Leavenworth, Kansas, on December 4, 1877. More than 431 surrendered, for some of the Indians died of wounds and exposure during their journey into exile. For details of the order to remove the Palouse and Nez Perce to the Indian Territory, see *Annual Report, SW*, 1876-77, p. 15. For the best discussion of the removal, see chapter 24 of Beal, *"I Will Fight No More Forever,"* and Brown, *Flight of the Nez Perce*, pp. 410-11.

[78] S.T.T. to editor, July 19, 1878, *Council Fire*, August, 1878.

[79] Ibid.

[80] Alan Osborne, "The Exile of the Nez Perce in Indian Territory, 1878-1885," *The Chronicles of Oklahoma* 56 ()1978-79); 453-58; *Annual Report of the Commissioner of Indian Affairs*, 1878, pp. 33-34.

[81] Whiteman to Hoyt, June 16, 1879, Office of Indian Affairs, Ponca Agency (PAO, NA, LR, File W-1388/1879.

[82] Husishusis Kute was considered the spiritual leader of the non-Christian Palouse and Nez Perce. When he returned to the Northwest, he first took a group of Indians to the Nez Perce Reservation in Idaho before joining other Palouses on the Colville Reservation in Washington. There he continued his religion and the Washani faith, commonly known as the Seven Drums, which is alive and a viable faith to this day.

[83] "Visit of Commissioners Fisk and Stickley to Colorado and Indian Territory," Tenth Annual Report of the Board of Indian Commissioners in 1878, p. 47, 51; "Speech of Senator Thomas C. McCreery on Transfer of Indian Department," February 10, 1879, *Congressional Record* 8 45th Cong., 3d Sess., pp. 1115-55; "Testimony of Chief Joseph, the Interpreter, and H.H. Gregg," October 7, 1878, *Senate Miscellaneous Documents* 45th Cong., 3d Sess., SS 1835.

[84] Washington, D.C., *Evening Star*, January 16, 1879; *Washington Post*, January 16, 1879.

[85] *Council Fire*, October 1879.

[86] Joseph, "An Indian's View of Indian Affairs." In May, 1879, a month after Joseph's article appeared, the *North American Review* carried a rebuttal by General Howard entitled "The True Story of the Wallowa Campaign."

[87] The influence of the article cannot be overstated. See Clark, "The Nez Perce in Exile," pp. 218-19, 228-29; Osborne, "The Exile of the Nez Perce," pp. 455-57, 468-70.

[88] *Council Fire*, October, 1879.

[89] McNeil to Hoyt, April 24, 1879, NA, OIA, Inspector's Files, M-989.

[90] *Council Fire*, June, 1883; Kate C. McBeth, *The Nez Perce Since Lewis and Clark* (New York, 1908), pp. 97-101.

[91] Fort Atkins' orders to return the Palouse and Nez Perce to the Northwest, see *House Executive Document* 88, 48th Cong., 2nd Sess., SS 2302; also see McBeth, *The Nez Perce Since Lewis and Clark*, pp. 97-101.

[92] Clark, "The Nez Perce in Exile," pp. 230-31; Chapman, "The Nez Perce in Indian Territory: An Archival Study," p. 121; Chappel, *The Nez Perce in Kay County, Oklahoma*, p. 5; McWhorter, *Yellow Wolf*, pp. 288-92.

[93] This essay appeared originally in the spring issue, 1985, of the *American Indian Quarterly* and is published here with the permission of the editor and the University of California, Berkeley. Oral interview by author, Richard Scheuerman, and Lee Ann Smith with Andrew George, November 15, 1980.

[94] Ibid. Andrew George's description of his family geneaology was confirmed by written documents. See "Nez Perce Reservation Allotment Book, prepared by Alice Fletcher, 1889-1892.:" The original is held by Ralph Wi lliams of Gifford, Idaho, but a microfilm copy (July, 1967) is found at the Idaho Historical Society in Boise, Idaho. Andrew's mother was Julia Johnson, Ipnowsietsan; his grandfather was Dick Johnson, Ipnamativekin; his father was Smith L. George. According to the documents, Andrew's maternal grandmother died at the age of 35 and her son Hencitstamat, died at the age of three. The last two individuals are buried in Oklahoma. The Palouse Indians lived along the Snake River in Washington. They were divided into three large groupings, including the Upper, Middle, and Lower bands. The Upper and some Middle Palouses engaged in the Nez Perce War and were removed to the Indian Territory.

[95] In *Renegade Tribe: The Palouse Indians and the Invasion of the Inland Pacific Northwest* (Pullman, Wa.: Washington State University Press, 1986), authors Clifford E. Trafzer and Richard Scheuerman detail the era of exploration, trade, and missions as they relate to the Palouses. For the treaty councils, see "Documents Relating to the Negotiation of Ratified and Unratified Treaties with Various Indian Tribes, 1801-69," National Archives, Records Group 75, Microfilm T494, Reel 5p hereafter cited as Walla Walla Council Proceedings. For the Yakima Treaty, see Charles J. Kappler, ed., *Indian Affairs, Laws and Treaties* 2 (Washington, 1904), pp. 694-705.

[96] There are numerous books and articles that examine the origins of the Nez Perce War, including Josephy, *The Nez Perce Indians;* Burns, *The Jesuits and the Indian Wars of the Northwest;* Kent D. Richards, *Issac I. Stevens: Young Man in a Hurry* (Provo, Utah, 1979); Beal, *"I Will Fight No More Forever";* McWhorter, *Hear Me,* and *Yellow Wolf;* Howard, *My Life and Experiences Among Our Hostile Indians* and *Nez Perce Joseph;* Joseph, "An Indian's View of Indian Affairs," pp. 412-33; Brown, *The Flight of the Nez Perce;* McDermott, *Forlorn Hope;* Haines, *The Nez Perces;* Kate McBeth, *The Nez Perce Since Lewis and Clark* (New York, 1908); Slickpoo, Noon Nee-Me-Poo; and Henry Clay Wood, The Status of Young Joseph and His Band of Nez Perce Indians (Portland, 1876).

[97] Josephy, *The Nez Perce,* pp. 391-426; see also the "Proceedings of the Treaty Council at Lapwai," National Archives, Record Group 75; McWhorter, *Yellow Wolf,* pp. 37-41; McWhorter, *Hear Me,* pp. 170-89; and Howard, **Nez Perce Joseph,** pp. 52-64; Camile W Williams to L.V. McWhorter, November 24, 1936, Box 211a, McWhorter Collection, Manuscripts and Archives, Washington State University, Pullman. In the same collection there are numerous statements regarding Husishusis Kute and Hahtalekin. See folders 211, p. 111; 213b, pp. 18,23,37,70; and 164, p. 12; h hereafter cited McWhorter Collection, WSU.

[98] Howard, *Nez Perce Joseph,* p. 64.

[99] Ibid., p. 64, 66.

[100] Ibid., p. 67.

[101] Burns, *The Jesuits and the Indian Wars*, pp. 393-98.

[102] Notes of L.V. McWhorter, folder 213b, pp. 23 and folder 164, p. 12, McWhorter Collection, WSU.

[103] McWhorter notes, folder 164, p. 12 and folder 213b, p. 235. Also see McWhorter, *Yellow Wolf*, p. 119.

[104] Josephy, *The Nez Perce*, pp. 626-32; see an eyewitness account of the surrender by Lieutenant C.E. S. Wood in Chester A. Fee, *Chief Joseph*, (New York, 1936), pp. 329-30; Brown, *Flight of the Nez Perce*, pp. 418-25; McWhorter, *Hear Me*, pp. 494-95; Beal, *"I Will Fight No More Forever*," p. 336.

[105] Sherman to Sheridan, August 31, 1877, Document Number 5588-77, National Archives, Adjutant Generals Office, 4364-77, as quoted in Beal, *"I Will Fight No More Forever*," pp. 297-98.

[106] Ibid., p. 257, 298-304; Josephy, *The Nez Perce*, pp. 631-33, 636-37; *Annual Report of the Commissioner of Indian Affairs*, 1878, quoting Hayt, p. 33; The Council Fire, August, 1878; McWhorter, *Hear Me*, pp. 529-30. The Palouse and the Nez Perce arrived at Fort Leavenworth on November 27, 1877. For an excellent account of the removal, see Steve Evans, unpublished manuscript, Department of History, Lewis and Clark State College, Lewiston, Idaho. President Rutherford B. Hayes and Secretary of Interior Carl Schurz asked Sherman to consider an investigation into the possible return of the Nez Perce and Palouse to the Northwest. Colonel Nelson A. Miles was in favor of the investigation but Generals Howard and McDowell vetoed the idea. No investigation was launched in 1878.

[107] *United States Statutes At Large* 20, p. 74.

[108] Baxter Springs, the headquarters of the Quapaw Agency, was located in the Kansas Territory not the Indian Territory. Clark, "The Nez Perces in Exile," *Pacific Northwest Quarterly*, p. 215; *Annual Report of the Commissioner of Indian Affairs*, 1878, p. 32.

[109] Testimony of H.H. Gregg, *Senate Miscellaneous Document* 53, 45th Cong., 3rd Sess., pp. 183-84; *Annual Report Of the Commissioner of Indian Affairs*, 1877, p. 409; Josephy, *The Nez Perce*, p. 638.

[110] *Annual Report of the Commissioner of Indian Affairs*, 1878, p. 34; Osborne, "The Exile of the Nez Perce in Indian Territory, 1878-1885," pp. 453-58; Proceedings of the Commissioner E.A. Hayt and Board of Commissioners with the Palouse and Nez Perce, *Senate Miscellaneous Documents* 53, 45th Cong., 3rd Sess., pp. 77-78; and Josephy, *The Nez Perce*, p. 639. The Poncas had only recently moved to their new reservation from the Quapaw Reservation. The Poncas had arrived on the Quapaw Reservation in July, 1876, and remained there until the summer of 1878 when they were moved to the Cherokee Outlet. See United States Statutes 20, Vol. 63, Act of May 27, 1878, p. 76. As early as 1873, the Bureau of Indian Affairs received complaints from its agents regarding the removal of northern tribes to the Indian Territory where the people sickened and died. According to the *Annual Report of the Commissioner of Indian Affairs*, 1873, pp. 5-6, "Experience has demonstrated the impolicy of sending northern Indians to the Indian Territory. To go no farther back than the date of the Pawnee removal, it will be seen that the effect of a radical change of climate is disastrous, as this tribe alone, in the first two years, lost by death over 800 out of its number of 2,376. The northern Cheyennes suffered severely, and the Poncas who were recently removed from contact with the unfriendly Sioux, and arrived there in July last, have already lost 36 by death, which, by an ordinary computation, would be the death-rate for the entire tribe for a period of four years."

[111] The basis work on the Washani Religion is Relander, *Drummers and Dreamers*. Recent scholarship by Margery Ann Beach Sharkey, "The Wanapums and the Priest Rapids Dam; Fulfillment of an Indian Prophecy," will be forthcoming in the *Pacific Northwest Quarterly*. See also James Mooney, "The Ghost Dance Religion," *Fourteenth Annual Report of the Bureau of American Ethnology*, 1892-93, pt. 2 (Washington, D.C. 1896), Chapter 7, pp. 716-45; Cora Du Bois, "The Feather Cult of the Middle Columbia," *General Series in Anthropology* 7 (Menasha, Wisc., 1938); Leslie Spier, "The Prophet Dance of the Northwest and its Derivatives: The Source of the Ghost Dance," *General Series in Anthropology* (Menasha, Wisc., 1935); E.L. Huggins, "Smohalla, The Prophet of Priest Rapids," *Overland Monthly* 17 (1891): 208-15; J.W. MacMurray, "The

'Dreamers' of the Columbia River Valley, in Washington Territory," *Transactions of the Albany Institute* 11 (1887); 241-48; G.B. Kuykendall, "Smohalla," unpublished manuscript, Relander Collection, Yakima Valley Regional Library, Yakima, Washington.

[112]*Washington Post,* January 16, 18, 1879; *Washington Evening Star,* January 16, 18, 1879; *Council Fire,* July, 1879; Berlin B. Chapman, "The Nez Perces in Indian Territory: An Archival Study," *Oregon Historical Quarterly* 1 (June, 1849): 114; Osborne, "The Exile of the Nez Perce in Indian Territory 1878-1885," pp. 455-57; and Clark, "The Nez Perces in Exile," p. 218. Chief Joseph was permitted to visit Washington, D.C., largely because of the effort of Indian Inspector John O'Neil.

[113] On June 14, 1883, the Cherokees conveyed a tract of land known as the Cherokee Outlet to the United States government. The land on the Ponca Reserve ceded to the Nez Perce and Palouse "consisted of Townships 25 and 26 North, Range 1 West, and Townships 25 and 26, Range 2 West." The Cherokee colony was headed by Colonel J.M. Bell, and he was forced off the land by federal troops. See Clark, "The Nez Perces in Exile," pp. 219-20; Report of Special Agent J.M. Haworth, June 25, 1879 to Commissioner of Indian Affairs E.A. Hayt, National Archives, Office of Indian Affairs, Quapaw Agency, H-895/1879, reprinted in Velma Nieberding, "The Nez Perce in the Quapaw Agency," *The Chronicles of Oklahoma.*

[114] Clark, "The Nez Perces in Exile," p. 221; Report of William Whiteman, August 31, 1879 in the *Annual Report of the Commissioner of Indian Affairs,"* 1879, p. 7; *Council Fire,* October, 1879. Malaria was a major killer as well as heart and lung diseases.

[115] Osborne, "The Exile of the Nez Perce in Indian Territory, 1878-1885," p. 458; Clark, "The Nez Perces in Exile," p. 227; Mc Beth, *The Nez Perce Since Lewis and Clark,* p. 96.

[116] Slickpoo, *Noon Nee-Me-Poo,* p. 195; Osborne, "The Exile of the Nez Perce in Indian Territory, 1878-1885," pp. 460-67; Clark, "The Nez Perces in Exile," p. 223; Chapman, "The Nez Perces in Indian Territory," p. 116; *Annual Report of the Commissioner of Indian Affairs,* 1879, pp. 100-81.

[117] *Annual Report of the Commissioner of Indian Affairs*, 1881, pp. 335-37; Clark, "The Nez Perce in Exile," pp. 224-25; Osborne, "The Exile of the Nez Perce in Indian Territory, 1878-1885," p. 461.

[118] Wood to Price, October 3 and November 1, 1882, National Archives, Office of Indian Affairs, as found in Clark, "The Nez Perce in Exile," p. 225; *Annual Report of the Commissioner of Indian Affairs*, 1882, pp. 136-37, 395. In 1882 the Nez Perce and Palouse produced a good crop of corn as well as 800 bushels of wheat and 600 tons of hay.

[119] Report of Lewellyn E. Woodin, August 10, 1883 in *Annual Report of the Commissioner of Indian Affairs*, 1883, p. 79.

[120] Report of John W. Scott, August 15, 1884 in *Annual Report of the Commissioner of Indian Affairs*, 1884, p. 89 and 133-34.

[121] Osborne, "The Exile of the Nez Perce in Indian Territory, 1878-1885," p. 464: Clark, "The Nez Perces in Exile," p. 227.

[122] Joseph, "An Indian's View of Indian Affairs," pp. 412-33; Alvin Josephy, Jr., "The Last Stand of Chief Joseph," *American Heritage* 9 (February, 1958): 80; Miles, *Personal Recollections and Observations of General Nelson A. Miles*, p. n277; Nelson A. Miles, "Chief Joseph's Surrender," *New York Tribune Supplement*, August 4, 1907.

[123] Clark, "The Nez Perces in Exile," pp. 226-27.

[124] Clark, "The Nez Perces in Exile," pp. 226-27.

[125] *Council Fire*, June, 1883; McBeth, *The Nez Perces*, pp. 99-101.

[126] Clark, "The Nez Perces in Exile," p. 229; *United States Statutes at Large* 23, pp. 19, 378.

127 Clark, "The Nez Perces in Exile," pp. 231-32; Osborne, "The Exile of the Nez Perce in Indian Territory, 1878-1885," p. 470; Josephy, *The Nez Perce*, pp. 641-42.

128 Deward E. Walker, Jr., *Conflict and Schism in Nez Perce Acculturation* (Pullman, Washington, 1968); Chappell, *The Nez Perce in Kay County, Oklahoma*, pp. 1-5.

129 The quote is from Slickpoo, *Noon Ne-me-poo*, p. 195; oral interview by author, Scheuerman, and Smith with Andrew George, November 15, 1980; Whitman to Trafzer, October 5, 1981, author's personal files. According to reports filed in the *Annual Report of the Commissioner of Indian Affairs*, 1885, pp. 71, 185-186, Husishusis Kute took the people to the Nez Perce Reservation in Idaho. However, he moved to the Colville Reservation and "he died in Nespelem, before Chief Joseph." Williams to McWhorter, November 24, 1936, McWhorter Collection, WSU.